CONGRESSIONAL POLICIES, PRACTICES AND PROCEDURES

COVERED BONDS: FEATURES AND PROPOSALS

CONGRESSIONAL POLICIES, PRACTICES AND PROCEDURES

Additional books in this series can be found on Nova's website under the Series tab.

Additional E-books in this series can be found on Nova's website under the E-books tab.

ECONOMIC ISSUES, PROBLEMS AND PERSPECTIVES

Additional books in this series can be found on Nova's website under the Series tab.

Additional E-books in this series can be found on Nova's website under the E-books tab.

CONGRESSIONAL POLICIES, PRACTICES AND PROCEDURES

COVERED BONDS: FEATURES AND PROPOSALS

WEI ZHAO
AND
CHAN LI
EDITORS

Nova Science Publishers, Inc.
New York

Copyright © 2011 by Nova Science Publishers, Inc.

All rights reserved. No part of this book may be reproduced, stored in a retrieval system or transmitted in any form or by any means: electronic, electrostatic, magnetic, tape, mechanical photocopying, recording or otherwise without the written permission of the Publisher.

For permission to use material from this book please contact us:
Telephone 631-231-7269; Fax 631-231-8175
Web Site: http://www.novapublishers.com

NOTICE TO THE READER

The Publisher has taken reasonable care in the preparation of this book, but makes no expressed or implied warranty of any kind and assumes no responsibility for any errors or omissions. No liability is assumed for incidental or consequential damages in connection with or arising out of information contained in this book. The Publisher shall not be liable for any special, consequential, or exemplary damages resulting, in whole or in part, from the readers' use of, or reliance upon, this material. Any parts of this book based on government reports are so indicated and copyright is claimed for those parts to the extent applicable to compilations of such works.

Independent verification should be sought for any data, advice or recommendations contained in this book. In addition, no responsibility is assumed by the publisher for any injury and/or damage to persons or property arising from any methods, products, instructions, ideas or otherwise contained in this publication.

This publication is designed to provide accurate and authoritative information with regard to the subject matter covered herein. It is sold with the clear understanding that the Publisher is not engaged in rendering legal or any other professional services. If legal or any other expert assistance is required, the services of a competent person should be sought. FROM A DECLARATION OF PARTICIPANTS JOINTLY ADOPTED BY A COMMITTEE OF THE AMERICAN BAR ASSOCIATION AND A COMMITTEE OF PUBLISHERS.

Additional color graphics may be available in the e-book version of this book.

Library of Congress Cataloging-in-Publication Data

Covered bonds : features and proposals / editors, Wei Zhao and Chan Li.
    p. cm.
  Includes bibliographical references and index.
  ISBN 978-1-61470-118-7 (hbk. : alk. paper) 1. Covered bonds--United States. 2. Mortgage-backed securities--United States. I. Zhao, Wei, 1962 Jan. 23- II. Li, Chan, 1971-
  HG5095.C78 2011
  332.63'23--dc23
                2011022178

Published by Nova Science Publishers, Inc. † New York

CONTENTS

Preface		**vii**
Chapter 1	Covered Bonds: Issues in the 112th Congress *Edward V. Murphy*	**1**
Chapter 2	Testimony of Scott A. Stengel, before the U.S. House Subcommittee on Capital Markets and Government Sponsored Enterprises, Hearing on "Legislative Proposals to Create a Covered Bond Market in the United States"	**21**
Chapter 3	Testimony of Bert Ely, before the U.S. House Subcommittee on Capital Markets and Government Sponsored Enterprises, Hearing on "Legislative Proposals to Create a Covered Bond Market in the United States"	**41**
Chapter 4	Statement of Tim Skeet, Board Member of the International Capital Market Association1, before the U.S. House Subcommittee on Capital Markets and Government Sponsored Enterprises, Hearing on "Legislative Proposals to Create a Covered Bond Market in the United States"	**61**
Chapter 5	Statement of Ralph Daloisio, Managing Director, Natixis, on behalf of the American Securitization Forum, ASF Covered Bonds Subforum, before the U.S. House Subcommittee on Capital Markets and Government Sponsored Enterprises, Hearing on	

	"Legislative Proposals to Create a Covered Bond Market in the United States"	79
Chapter 6	Testimony of Stephen G. Andrews, Bank of Alameda, before the U.S. House Subcommittee on Capital Markets and Government Sponsored Enterprises, Hearing on "Legislative Proposals to Create a Covered Bond Market in the United States"	95
Chapter 7	Statement of the Federal Deposit Insurance Corporation, before the U.S. House Subcommittee on Capital Markets and Government Sponsored Enterprises, Hearing on "Legislative Proposals to Create a Covered Bond Market in the United States"	101
Chapter 8	Best Practices for Residential Covered Bonds *The Department of the Treasury*	113
Chapter Sources		143
Index		145

PREFACE

This book examines the features and proposals of residential covered bond utilization and future issues for the 112th Congress. Covered bonds are a relatively common method of funding mortgages in Europe, however uncommon in the United States. A covered bond is a recourse debt obligation that is secured by a pool of assets, often mortgages. The holders of the bond are given additional protection in the event of bankruptcy or insolvency of the issuing lender. Because some believe that the subprime mortgage turmoil may have been influenced by poor incentives for lenders using the securitization process, some policymakers have recommended covered bonds as an alternative for U.S. mortgage markets. Although covered bond contracts are not prohibited in the U.S., some policymakers believe that legislation and agency rulemaking could facilitate the growth of a domestic covered bond market.

Chapter 1- Covered bonds are a relatively common method of funding mortgages in Europe, but uncommon in the United States. A covered bond is a recourse debt obligation that is secured by a pool of assets, often mortgages. The holders of the bond are given additional protection in the event of bankruptcy or insolvency of the issuing lender. Covered bonds have some features, such as pooled mortgages, that resemble securitization, but the original lenders maintain a continuing interest in the performance of the loans. Because some believe that the subprime mortgage turmoil may have been influenced by poor incentives for lenders using the securitization process, some policymakers have recommended covered bonds as an alternative for U.S. mortgage markets. Although covered bond contracts are not prohibited in the United States, some policymakers believe that legislation and agency rulemaking could facilitate the growth of a domestic covered bond market.

Chapter 2- I am a partner in the Washington, D.C., office of King & Spalding LLP and a member of the Steering Committee for the U.S. Covered Bond Council (the Council). The Council is a collaborative forum comprised of investors, issuers, dealers, and other participants in the covered-bond market, and we strive to develop policies and practices that harmonize the views of these different constituencies and that promote a vibrant market for U.S. covered bonds.[1]

Chapter 3- The covered bond concept is quite simple. Essentially, covered bonds are debt instruments issued by a bank or any other type of financial firm which are secured by assets owned outright by the issuer. The bonds also are a direct liability of the issuer, which provides a second source of repayment should the assets securing the covered bonds be insufficient to provide for repayment. In this regard, covered bonds differ sharply from asset securitization wherein assets are sold to a bankruptcy-remote trust which then issues debt securities of various types and tranches to pay for the purchase of those assets.

Chapter 4- This testimony provides an overview of the European covered bond market, and is the result of discussions with various European stakeholders, in particular the International Capital Market Association ('ICMA') and one of the Association's subcommittees, which was created nearly two years ago as the Covered Bond Investor Council ('CBIC'). This Council serves to consider issues related to the evolution of the product in Europe and the type of information available to investors. We have also liaised closely in the preparation of this paper with the European Covered Bond Council ('ECBC')[2], which represents a wide group of market participants.

Chapter 5- The American Securitization Forum (the "ASF") was formed to enable participants in the US securitization industry to pursue a mission of education, consensus, and advocacy on matters relating to the form and function of the US securitized debt capital markets. The ASF has over 330 institutional members engaged in every significant aspect of this market— issuers, investors, servicers, dealers, ratings agencies, law firms, trustees, and a variety of data and technology vendors. Assuming a legislated US covered bond market is established, our members will have a leading and lasting role in this new financial instrument, much like they did over 25 years ago with the creation of the first asset-backed security.

Chapter 6- I am pleased to present testimony raising several serious concerns and objections about the possible development of a covered bond market in the United States (U.S.). To cut to the chase, speaking from my perspective as a community banker, I do not think that we as a country need to expend the time, energy and resources to attempt to create a covered bond market in the U.S. In my opinion, and I believe that I am supported in this view by Treasury Secretary Geithner, wealready have a covered bond market: it is the Federal Home Loan Bank System. I am a member of the Federal Home Loan Bank of San Francisco. We do not need to try to import from Europe an experimental housing finance tool that would be deployed under greatly different conditions and circumstances and as far as I can see would largely benefit the biggest banks in the industry.

Chapter 7- The FDIC appreciates the opportunity to provide its views on the regulatory and legislative issues posed by covered bonds. The FDIC has long worked with the financial industry to establish a sound foundation for a vibrant covered bond market that will provide U.S. banks with an additional source of liquidity. These efforts include working with the first U.S. banks to issue covered bonds in 2006 and the FDIC's adoption in July 2008, of a Statement of Policy on the treatment of covered bonds to clarify key issues related to deposit insurance and bank resolutions. Our efforts facilitated the creation of a market-tested and market-accepted covered bond program for U.S. banks that meets investors' needs without increasing the government's exposure to this investment class.

Chapter 8- This Best Practices guide has been prepared by the Department of the Treasury ("Treasury") in order to encourage the growth of the Covered Bond market in the United States. Treasury believes that Covered Bonds represent a potential additional source of financing that could reduce borrowing costs for homeowners, improve liquidity in the residential mortgage market, and help depository institutions strengthen their balance sheets by diversifying their funding sources.

In: Covered Bonds: Features and Proposals ISBN: 978-1-61470-118-7
Editors: Wei Zhao and Chan Li © 2011 Nova Science Publishers, Inc.

Chapter 1

COVERED BONDS:
ISSUES IN THE 112ᵀᴴ CONGRESS[*]

Edward V. Murphy

SUMMARY

Covered bonds are a relatively common method of funding mortgages in Europe, but uncommon in the United States. A covered bond is a recourse debt obligation that is secured by a pool of assets, often mortgages. The holders of the bond are given additional protection in the event of bankruptcy or insolvency of the issuing lender. Covered bonds have some features, such as pooled mortgages, that resemble securitization, but the original lenders maintain a continuing interest in the performance of the loans. Because some believe that the subprime mortgage turmoil may have been influenced by poor incentives for lenders using the securitization process, some policymakers have recommended covered bonds as an alternative for U.S. mortgage markets. Although covered bond contracts are not prohibited in the United States, some policymakers believe that legislation and agency rulemaking could facilitate the growth of a domestic covered bond market.

In some countries, covered bonds conforming to statutorily prescribed features may receive enhanced protections or greater regulatory certainty. A statutory framework for covered bonds often

---

[*] This is an edited, reformatted and augmented version of a Congressional Research Service publication, CRS Report for Congress R41322, from www.crs.gov, dated March 4, 2011.

includes four elements: (1) the bond is issued by (or bondholders otherwise have full recourse to) a credit institution that is subject to public supervision and regulation; (2) bondholders have a claim against a cover pool of financial assets in priority to the unsecured creditors of the credit institution; (3) the credit institution has the ongoing obligation to maintain sufficient assets in the cover pool to satisfy the claims of covered bondholders at all times; and (4) in addition to general supervision of the issuing institution, public or other independent bodies supervise the institution's specific obligations to the covered bonds. Some analysts include the presence of such a statutory framework in the definition of a covered bond, in which case there have not been any covered bonds issued in the United States (and many so-called covered bonds issued elsewhere would also no longer be rightfully called covered bonds).

Compared with securitization, covered bonds may be less susceptible to poor underwriting standards because issuers maintain risk exposure or "skin in the game," perhaps minimizing problems of the "originate to distribute" model of lending. Institutions that issue covered bonds may be less susceptible to investor panic because the status of covered bonds on their balance sheet is transparent. On the other hand, reliance on covered bonds may reduce aggregate lending because it ties up more capital than does securitization.

Potentially, there could be some regulatory uncertainty on the treatment of holders of covered bonds when the Federal Deposit Insurance Corporation (FDIC) places banks in receivership or conservatorship. To address some of these concerns, the FDIC issued two policy statements in 2008, Financial Institution Letter (FIL) 34-2008 and FIL 73-2008, clarifying its obligations to the holders of covered bonds if an FDIC-insured institution is placed in FDIC receivership or conservatorship. Because the use of covered bonds in the United States is rare, there is still little experience in actually resolving a covered bond.

INTRODUCTION

Covered bonds are one method for financial institutions to raise funds from investors. They are rare in the United States, although variations of covered bonds have been used in Europe for centuries. Although covered bonds are not a prohibited form of debt contract in the United States, some observers believe that legislation and agency rulemaking is required to facilitate the growth of a larger domestic covered bond market.

Policymakers are considering increased reliance on covered bonds as an alternative to securitization. This report discusses various definitions of covered bonds, analyzes some of the economic advantages and disadvantages of this funding mechanism compared with securitization, and summarizes recent legislative proposals.

DEFINITIONS

Conceptually, a covered bond is a way for financial institutions to raise funds by offering collateral to investors. A bank sells a bond to investors, and the bond is backed both by the bank's promise to repay and by the assets pledged as collateral.[1] It is important to distinguish between the debt that serves as the collateral and the debt that is the bond itself. A covered bond is a debt in which a financial institution is the borrower. The primary collateral backing the covered bond is also debt, often mortgages in which the financial institution was the lender or has a close relationship with the lender. A covered bond typically uses mortgages (or other debt) as collateral for a bond that a financial institution sells to investors.

It is difficult to present a single technical definition of existing covered bonds because variations of this debt contract have been used in many European countries for centuries. In some countries, variations of covered bonds can be constructed through private contract. In other countries, covered bonds conforming to statutorily prescribed features may receive enhanced protections. For such statutorily protected covered bonds, according to the European Central Bank (ECB), the closest thing to a shared definition is European Covered Bond Council's "essential features of covered bonds," which includes four elements: (1) the bond is issued by (or bondholders otherwise have full recourse to) a credit institution which is subject to public supervision and regulation; (2) bondholders have a claim against a cover pool of financial assets in priority to the unsecured creditors of the credit institution; (3) the credit institution has the ongoing obligation to maintain sufficient assets in the cover pool to satisfy the claims of covered bondholders at all times; and (4) the obligations of the credit institution in respect of the cover pool are supervised by public or other independent bodies.[2] If that definition is accepted, then no U.S. covered bonds are actually covered bonds because the United States does not as yet have an independent cover pool supervisor.

A comparison to other sources of funds for financial institutions may be helpful in understanding covered bonds. A distinguishing feature of a covered bond is that it is dual-recourse, which means that the investor has recourse against both the financial institution selling the bond and the pool of assets backing the bond.[3] In contrast, a bank or other financial institution could offer a bond with no collateral, in which case the bond is a form of unsecured debt. Alternatively, the financial institution could sell the underlying loans to an independent collateral pool that serves as the only backing of the bond, in which case the bond is a typical American private-label asset-backed security (ABS). If backed by mortgages, the ABS is a mortgage-backed security (MBS). Table 1 compares the typical covered bond structures to unsecured debt and ABS or MBS. Variations on the general structures are presented in the table, for example, Fannie Mae and Freddie Mac (the government-sponsored enterprises, GSEs) typically guarantee credit risk for their MBS. Note that Table 1 is a general description; it is possible to design ABS and covered bonds in which there is a claim against the issuing financial institutions for some kinds of risks but not for others.

Table 1. Investor Recourse for Selected Financial Institution Funding Sources

		Claim Against Collateral Pool	
		No	Yes
Claim Against Financial Institution	No		Private-Label ABS and MBS
	Yes	Unsecured Debt	Covered Bond GSE MBS

Source: Covered Bonds in the EU Financial System, available at
http://www.ecb.int/pub/pdf/other/coverbondsintheeufinancialsystem200812en_en.pdf.

American banks are not prohibited from using the covered bond contract to raise funds, although there are few American covered bonds. In practice, the Federal Deposit Insurance Corporation (FDIC) may have the ability to limit the market for covered bonds through its regulatory power over insured depositories. For example, the FDIC can limit the type of collateral that may be used or the percent of the depository's balance sheet that is funded with covered bonds. The FDIC defined covered bonds in FIL 73-2008 on August 4, 2008. The policy statement defines a covered bond as:

> a non-deposit, recourse debt obligation of an IDI [Insured depository Institution] with a term greater than one year and no more than thirty years, that is secured directly or indirectly by perfected security interests under applicable state and federal law on assets held and owned by the IDI consisting of eligible mortgages, or AAA-rated mortgage-backed securities secured by eligible mortgages if for no more than ten percent of the collateral for any covered bond issuance or series.[4]

Covered Bonds: Issues in the 112th Congress

Table 2. Comparing the Structure of Securitization and Covered Bonds

	Private Securitization	Covered Bonds
Structure	Issuer gathers mortgages (or other assets) from one or more banks in a pool and sells securities which represent claims on the cash flow of the pool.	A bank puts its own mortgages (or other assets) in a pool, sells interest in the pool, and stands ready to cover losses if the pool does not perform.
Claims of bondholders against mortgage pool	Bondholders have claim against mortgages in pool.	Bondholders have claim against mortgages in pool.
Claims of bondholders against loan originator	Bondholders do not have claim against other assets of loan originators (assuming the issuer does not provide credit enhancement).	If mortgage pool exhausted, bondholders retain claim against loan originator.
Balance sheet treatment	Usually NOT recorded as a liability of the loan originator or securities issuer.	Usually recorded as a liability of the loan originator or covered bond issuer.
Loan originator record of sale on assets	Gain on sale when sold to trust, subject to accounting standards.	The mortgages are not sold so no gain to record.
Servicing the loan	Originators sold the loans so servicing is an independent relationship, but originator can service loan under contract.	No isolation of originator from mortgage assets, so servicing relationship unaffected.
Originator bankruptcy	Mortgages in the pool are remote from bankruptcy of the loan originator.	Bondholders have full claims on mortgages in pool even if loan originator is in insolvency proceedings.
Ratings agencies	Assess only the risk of the assets and credit enhancement in the mortgage pool.	Must assess risk of assets in pool but also the risk of the issuing bank as a whole.

Because securitization is more common than covered bonds in the United States, it may be helpful to compare typical features of private securitization to typical features of covered bonds. As discussed above, covered bonds are supported by both the pledged mortgages (or other assets) and the issuing bank, but there are other elements of interest to some policymakers (discussed in more detail below). For example, covered bonds typically remain on the balance sheet of sponsoring institutions while securitized assets typically do not. Therefore, covered bonds typically tie up more capital than typical securitizations. On the other hand, issuers of covered bonds typically have more long-term stake in the performance of the assets in the cover pool than typical securitization. Table 2 compares selected features of covered bonds to typical private securitization of U.S. mortgages.

POLICY ISSUES

The steep drop in the volume of securitization and the rising cost of GSE intervention have encouraged some policymakers to consider alternative funding sources for mortgage finance. Covered bonds might be less subject to investor loss of confidence than securitization because covered bond issuers maintain a long-term interest in the underlying loans and because the exposure of banks to covered bonds remains recorded on their balance sheets.[5] These potential advantages would have to be weighed against less advantageous capital requirements for issuing institutions and potential costs to the FDIC's deposit insurance fund. Some potential economic benefits and costs of covered bonds are presented below.

"Skin in the Game" and Underwriting

The foreclosure crisis has caused some to question the long-term incentives of securitization. In securitization, lenders sell their loans to the secondary market. Because institutions in the primary mortgage market do not retain risk of borrower default, that is, do not have "skin in the game," there may not be a sufficient check against eroding underwriting standards.[6]

An alternative approach would be to mandate that issuers in securitization retain some pre-specified amount of risk. A potential downside of this approach is that it might encourage the creation of more complex financial instruments. Mandating that banks retain only a part of risk requires the creation of instruments that can divide the risk between the issuers and the holders of the securities. Regulators are charged with making sure that the portion of risk being retained by the issuer is not being hedged, because hedging would defeat the purpose of the retained risk regulation. Securities issuers still want to avoid risk, so they would have an incentive to create complex instruments that complicate regulators' efforts to monitor their retained risk and hedging activities.

Advocates of covered bonds point out that the issuers maintain a long term stake in the performance of the loans.[7] If the underlying loans default, the financial institution is still responsible for payments to the holders of the covered bonds. By its nature, a covered bond requires issuers to have 100% skin in the game, which presumably encourages the maintenance of quality underwriting standards.

The distinction between statutory and contractual covered bonds allows for further refinement. Recall that a covered bond contract is not currently prohibited, which in theory means that firms can offer a variety of covered bond structures. In practice, financial regulatory agencies could limit the collateral eligible for covered bonds issued by regulated institutions. Similarly, Congress could enact a statutory framework that limits the collateral eligible for covered bonds by any or all lenders. A statutory framework for covered bonds, or for securitization, could limit eligible collateral to loans with quality underwriting. The FDIC has issued related guidance and there is a proposal in Congress to enact a statutory framework for covered bonds (discussed below).

Transparency and Investor Confidence

The complexity of asset securitization may have contributed to financial market turmoil and panic. For investors evaluating firms that had issued securitized assets, it was not always clear if issuers would have to support the securities they had sold that were off the current balance sheet (a contingent liability). For investors evaluating the securities themselves, the complexities of MBS construction may have made it difficult to estimate the current value of the securities or anticipate write-downs by institutions holding them. The loss of investor confidence may have been exacerbated by lack of transparency of securitized mortgages.

Advocates of covered bonds argue that they have a financial structure that is more transparent than securitization.[8] Balance sheets of covered bond issuers may more accurately reflect risks because the issuers of covered bonds do not sell the assets. Investors evaluating the health of covered bond issuers are less likely to be surprised by a contingent liability of the issuer because the issuer has already disclosed a promise to support the bonds. Similarly, the typical covered bond transaction is less likely than securitization to issue multiple classes of complex securities from the same underlying loan pool because the issuer is promising to pay investors anyway. Here again, regulatory agencies and Congress have the option to further encourage transparency by creating a statutory framework, although in theory similar revisions could be done to support transparency in securitization.

Capital Requirements and Lending Volume

Regulatory agencies encouraged securitization in the 1990s, in part because this was believed to transfer default risk out of the banking system.[9] Bank regulations allowed securitizers to reduce capital because the loans were typically sold off the balance sheet of the issuer.[10] Therefore, securitization may have enabled a higher volume of lending for a given amount of capital in the banking system. Policymakers considering a future shift from securitization to covered bonds would have to take into account the advantages and disadvantages of higher potential capital requirements and lower lending volume.

Like securitization, covered bonds essentially allow lenders to access investors in the secondary market without necessarily obtaining capital from them. In other words, the sale of a covered bond does not itself add capital to the balance sheet of a covered bond issuer, just as the sale of a MBS does not itself add capital to an MBS issuer. Unlike securitization, investors in covered bonds have recourse against the covered bond issuer. Therefore, issuers of covered bonds would have more risk than sellers of MBS, and would have to hold more risk-based capital to support the funding of the same volume of lending, all else equal. As a result, a shift to covered bonds could require either more resources to be held as capital in the banking system, or less overall lending, or some combination of the two.

Policymakers could change the relative capital treatment of securitized assets and covered bonds. Financial regulatory agencies have altered the accounting treatment of certain securitized assets, which could reduce the relative advantage of securitization. For example, FDIC guidance on Financial Accounting Standards (FAS) 166 and 167 could result in securitizers retaining more capital than under prior accounting rules.[11] To the extent recent regulatory actions may increase capital requirements under securitization, the relative capital disadvantage of covered bonds may decline in the near future.

Maturity Mismatch

In banking, maturity generally refers to the length of time that a borrower has to repay the loan.[12] In general, much of a bank's liabilities are short-term instruments. For example, customer deposits are subject to immediate withdrawal on demand. However, many of a bank's assets have a longer maturity, such as 30-year fixed-rate mortgages. This general bank structure has a maturity mismatch, which exposes the banking system to potential problems when interest rates unexpectedly suffer extreme fluctuations. One perceived advantage of securitization was that it allowed banks to sell their long-term assets, and thus potentially better cope with the maturity of mortgages and similar assets.[13] Under securitization, a bank (which has short maturity liabilities) could sell a mortgage (a long maturity asset) to an insurance company (with long maturity liabilities) or other investors with tolerance for long-maturity assets.

Covered bonds are an intermediate case between funding loans held in portfolio through deposits and funding loans through securitization. Unlike securitization, covered bonds do not remove long-maturity assets from the issuer's balance sheet. Instead, a covered bond allows a bank to fund itself with a long-maturity liability. By matching long-term assets with long-term liabilities, covered bonds potentially allow banks to reduce maturity mismatch compared with portfolio lending funded solely through deposits and other short-term liabilities. However, a bank that issues a covered bond backed by a pool of mortgages must still cope with some maturity mismatch because the actual maturity of some loans, such as mortgages, is of uncertain length. For example, people might prepay their mortgage when they move. Therefore, an increased reliance on covered bonds rather than securitization might increase maturity-mismatch risks in the banking system to the degree that financial institutions cannot forecast the actual maturity of their loans. This might cause some institutions to increase their use of financial derivatives, which raise issues of transparency and risk themselves, if covered bonds were to replace securitization.

Failing Depositories and the Deposit Insurance Fund

The FDIC resolves failing banks with insured deposits. Once an institution has been seized by the FDIC, the greater the proceeds from the sale of its assets the smaller the potential loss to the FDIC's Deposit Insurance Fund

(DIF). Generally, the FDIC has a superior claim to assets of failing banks. However, the point of covered bonds is generally to promote bondholder interests should the issuer fail to make the covered bond payments. Were the FDIC to minimize investor rights to collateral for failing banks, the market would probably find it difficult to sell covered bonds in the future. Because covered bonds are rare in the United States, some investors might want greater clarity regarding FDIC policies should a covered bond issuer fail. How will the FDIC treat investors in covered bonds should an issuer fail, and how might an increase in covered bonds affect the DIF?

Policymakers can protect the FDIC's DIF in any of a number of ways. For example, the amount of covered bonds that each institution could issue could be limited to a small portion of its overall balance sheet. Alternatively, investors in covered bonds could be put on notice that the FDIC has additional directives to protect the DIF should the fund run low. The FDIC could be directed to only recognize investor security interests in covered bonds after it is clear that there will be no drain on the DIF. If any of these options are chosen, economic theory predicts that the price investors would be willing to pay for a covered bond would reflect the decreased risk adjusted recovery of the bond. That is, banks might get slightly lower revenues from issuing covered bonds when healthy, and investors would get lower recovery rates on covered bonds should a bank fail.

Alternatively, policymakers could choose to promote covered bonds relative to the DIF. For example, legislation could direct the FDIC to respect covered bond claims even at the expense of the DIF. Should this or a similar option be chosen, economic theory predicts that banks would generally get slightly higher revenues from issuing covered bonds in good times, and investors would get higher recovery rates on covered bonds should a bank fail. If policymakers choose to promote covered bonds relative to the DIF then a potential future wave of bank failures might cause greater losses for taxpayers were the DIF to run out and the FDIC tap its line of credit with the Treasury.

Comparison to Federal Home Loan Bank Advances

Covered bonds have some characteristics in common with the Federal Home Loan Bank (FHLB) system. Like covered bonds, FHLB loans to their member institutions are dual recourse. Members of a regional FHLB pledge mortgages as collateral for FHLB loans, called advances. When member institutions fail, the regional FHLB gets paid before many other creditors of the bank. This repayment priority at the time of failure is called a superlien. The superlien is not only the pledged mortgages, rather the superlien can draw on the entire balance sheet of the financial institution. The net effect of requiring members to pledge the mortgages as collateral for the advances is to create a practical constraint on the volume of advances that any member institution can obtain (in addition to any other regulatory constraints). In practice, because money is easily transferrable, FHLB advances can be used to fund non-mortgage activities as long as the total volume of advances does not exceed the institution's holdings of mortgages.[14]

Some of these FHLB advance features resemble covered bonds. For example, both covered bonds and FHLB advances allow creditors to the financial institution to improve their priority in repayment should the firm fail. Both allow the mortgage originator to keep the funded mortgage on its own balance sheet, which can improve transparency. FHLBs monitor their members, which has some similarities to a public or independent monitor of the cover pool.

There are important differences between covered bonds and FHLB advances. A holder of a covered bond does not have recourse against the entire balance sheet of the financial institution; rather the holder of the covered bond has recourse to specific assets. Note that the issuer of the covered bond has some duties to maintain the value of the cover pool. The capital requirements for covered bonds need not be the same as capital requirements for FHLB advances. In many cases, FHLB advances are callable.

AGENCY ACTIONS ON COVERED BONDS

In response to mortgage market turmoil in 2007 and 2008, the Treasury Department and the FDIC considered rulemaking to encourage the use of covered bonds as an alternative to mortgage securitization. They believed that covered bonds might be a more stable source of funding than securitization because the volume of American private-label mortgage securitizations collapsed as mortgage market turmoil progressed.[15]

Treasury Proposals and Best Practices

Proposals for facilitating covered bonds were not merely a reaction to the financial panic of September 2008. Covered bonds were being discussed prior to the Lehman Brothers bankruptcy. Following mortgage market turmoil in the summer of 2007, Treasury officials were concerned that investor confidence in the securitization of mortgages might not be sustainable under mortgage market conditions prevailing at that time. On March 13, 2008, Treasury officials suggested the increased use of covered bonds as one option to restore confidence in mortgage finance:

> Covered bonds, which allow banks to retain originated mortgage loans while accessing financial market funding, are another alternative worth considering. Covered bonds may address the current lack of liquidity in, and bring more competition to, mortgage securitization. Rule-making, not legislation, is needed to facilitate the issuance of covered bonds. Through clarification of covered bonds' status in the event of a bank-issuer's insolvency, the FDIC can reduce uncertainty and consider appropriate measures that will protect the deposit insurance fund. These steps would encourage a covered bond market in the U.S.; similar changes in Europe have resulted in more covered bond activity.[16]

In an effort to provide clarity to the U.S. covered bond market, the Treasury Department issued a *Best Practices for Residential Covered Bonds* document on July 28, 2008.[17] This guide was designed to function as a complement to the FDIC's April 30 and August 4, 2008, policy statements on covered bonds (discussed below), and it was developed through consultation with the FDIC, the Federal Reserve, the Office of the Comptroller of the Currency, the Office of Thrift Supervision, and the Securities and Exchange Commission, as well as with international financial regulators and a variety of market participants. In particular, the Treasury Department outlined numerous standards for covered bond programs to follow in order to be consistent with this *Best Practices* template, including that (1) issuers be either newly created bankruptcy-remote special purpose vehicles or depository institutions; (2) the maturity for covered bonds be greater than one year, and no more than 30 years; (3) issuers hold an overcollateralization value of at least 5% of the outstanding covered bond principal balance; (4) the covered bonds not account for greater than 4% of an issuer's liabilities after issuance; and (5) each covered bond issued have a specified investment contract.[18]

FDIC Financial Institution Letters

In the United States, the FDIC resolves financial problems of failing banks with insured deposits. To adapt covered bonds to the U.S. system, therefore, FDIC rules for resolving claims against insolvent banks that have outstanding covered bonds might have to be modified. The FDIC issued Financial Institution Letters (FIL) on covered bonds in 2008 (FIL 34-2008 and FIL 73-2008) that apply to insured depository institutions (IDI).[19] The FDIC's final policy statement (73-2008) defined a covered bond as "a nondeposit, recourse debt obligation of an IDI with a term greater than one year and less than 30 years that is secured, directly or indirectly, by perfected security interests under applicable state and federal law on assets held and owned by the IDI consisting of eligible mortgages or, not exceeding 10 percent of the collateral for any covered bond issuance or series, AAA-rated mortgage-backed securities secured by eligible mortgages."[20] This definition may have limited the scope of covered bonds by U.S. banks to mortgage assets. Eligible mortgages include those that conform to agency guidance, including guidances on subprime and nontraditional mortgages.

FIL 73-2008 addressed the FDIC's intended policy should an insured depository fail. The FDIC noted that any liquidation of collateral of an IDI placed into conservatorship or receivership requires the consent of the FDIC during the initial 45 days or 90 days after its appointment, respectively. Consequently, issuers of covered bonds could incur additional costs from maintaining additional liquidity needed to insure continued payment on outstanding bonds if the FDIC as conservator or receiver were to fail to make payments or to provide access to the pledged collateral during these periods after any decision by the FDIC to terminate the covered bond transaction.

FDIC treatment of covered bonds was also an issue for financial market intervention after the Panic of 2008. On January 16, 2009, the FDIC announced that it would propose rule changes to its Temporary Liquidity Guarantee Program (TLGP) that extended the maturity of guarantee for some assets from three years to 10 years.[21] Because covered bonds possess longer maturities, this announcement was perceived as a move by the FDIC to accommodate this type of senior unsecured bank debt under the TLGP.[22] However, in May 2009, it was reported that FDIC Chairwoman Sheila Bair had decided to delay the implementation of this initiative.[23]

PERFORMANCE IN EUROPE DURING THE FINANCIAL CRISIS

In contrast to the United States, the European Union (EU) covered bond market has been a traditional feature of Europe's capital markets. As of the end of 2008, there was approximately 2.38 trillion euros in outstanding EU covered bonds.[24] There are various kinds of covered bonds in the EU market, but they can be categorized into two main types: regulated and structured. Regulated covered bonds are governed by specific legislation, including European directives, national legislation, and secondary legislation. Structured covered bonds operate outside any dedicated laws.[25] This distinction between regulated and structured European covered bonds is important because regulated covered bonds are subject to privileged financial market regulation, whereas their structured counterparts are not. Within the EU regulatory framework, two primary laws outlining the minimum requirements for a regulated covered bond are Article 22(4) of the 1988 Directive on Undertakings for Collective Investments in Transferable Securities (UCITS), and the Capital Requirements Directive (CRD).[26]

Because of global financial market instability, covered bonds have received significant attention from the European Central Bank (ECB). In particular, the ECB's Banking Supervision Committee (BSC) released a study in December 2008, *Covered Bonds in the EU Financial System*, which examined the impact of covered bonds on the stability of the EU financial system.[27] The BSC concluded in its report that EU covered bonds appeared relatively resilient to the recent global financial market turmoil, although covered bonds were adversely affected following the intensification of financial turbulence in September 2008. In an effort to assist European capital markets, the ECB in July 2009 began a one-year purchase program of approximately EUR 60 billion in covered bonds in both primary and secondary markets.[28]

The overall covered bond market in Europe has fared better than the American private label- mortgage securitization market. For example, the average spread between the average covered bond yield and euro interest rate swap rate remained relatively stable (between 90 and 100 basis points) after the finalization of the December 2009 FSR to end-April 2010. The debt crisis in some European countries is having a negative effect, however, as evidenced by spreads of covered bonds widened considerably in some euro area countries after May 2010.[29]

Appendix. Legislation in the 111TH Congress

Representative Garrett introduced three versions of a covered bonds bill in the 111th Congress. Representatives Kanjorski and Bachus cosponsored each bill. H.R. 2896, the Equal Treatment for Covered Bonds Act of 2009, was introduced on June 16, 2009.[30] This bill was followed by a proposal for a more detailed statutory framework for the regulation of covered bonds, H.R. 4884, the United States Covered Bond Act of 2010, introduced on March 18, 2010. H.R. 5823, also entitled the United States Covered Bond Act of 2010, was introduced on July 22, 2010, and marked up by the House Financial Services Committee on July 29, 2010.

H.R. 2896: Equal Treatment of Covered Bonds Act of 2009

The Equal Treatment of Covered Bonds Act of 2009, H.R. 2896, defined covered bonds and established regulatory authority among the banking agencies. H.R. 2896 amended the Federal Deposit Insurance Act (U.S.C. 1818(e)(3)(C)) to include a definition of a covered bond, which was " ... a nondeposit recourse debt obligation of an insured depository institution, with a term to maturity of at least 1 year, which is secured by specifically identified assets which are performing in accordance with the terms of the contracts which created the assets." H.R. 2896 specified actual direct compensatory damages that apply to covered bonds should a conservator or receiver be appointed for an issuer. It required joint rulemaking by the Secretary of the Treasury, the Board of Governors of the Federal Reserve System, the Comptroller of the Currency, the Director of the Office of Thrift Supervision, and the Board of Directors of the Federal Deposit Insurance Corporation. H.R. 2896 might have provided investors with greater certainty for how covered bonds would be treated should an institution fail and which agencies would make regulations; however, H.R. 2896 did not contain a requirement for an independent monitor of covered bond pools or a regulated covered bond program that are part of the European Covered Bond Council's (ECBC's) definition of a statutory framework for covered bonds.

H.R. 4884: United States Covered Bonds Act of 2010

In addition to defining covered bonds and designating authority to regulate covered bonds, H.R. 4884 contained provisions that would meet the ECBC's definition of statutory covered bonds. It requires independent cover pool monitors and a regulator for covered bonds. H.R. 4884 defined a covered bond as "any senior recourse debt obligation of an eligible issuer that: (A) has an original term to maturity of not less than 1 year; (B) is secured directly or indirectly by a perfected security interest in a cover pool which is owned directly or indirectly by the issuer of the obligation; (C) is issued under a covered bond program that has been approved by the covered bond regulator and is identified in a register of covered bonds maintained by the covered bond regulator; and (D) is not a deposit (as defined in section 3 of the Federal Deposit Insurance Act)." H.R. 4884 specified the Treasury as the covered bond regulator directed to approve covered bond programs.

H.R. 4884 would have allowed U.S. banks to issue covered bonds backed by a variety of asset classes, including asset-backed securities (ABSs), but specified minimum requirements for each asset class. Generally, H.R. 4884 specified that loan collateral in each asset class (mortgage, auto loan, etc.) would have to conform with existing regulatory guidances for loans in that asset class. If ABSs form the collateral for the covered bond, then the securities would have to be of the highest investment grade. For example, a commercial mortgage covered bond could have a pool of eligible commercial mortgage assets that complies with current bank regulator supervisory guidance or commercial mortgage-backed securities (CMBS) of the highest investment grade. Minimum standards were also specified for residential mortgages, home equity loans, public sector loans (including state and municipal), auto loans, credit cards, student loans, small business loans, and any other asset class that the covered bond regulator (Treasury) were to designate.

Covered bond programs would have been subject to a number of requirements. Each institution's program would have to be approved and registered. The cost of registration and regulation would be covered by fees on covered bond programs. Covered bonds issued by an approved program would be subject to minimum overcollateralization requirements and asset-coverage tests. Covered bonds would not be allowed to combine asset classes (auto loans and student loans, for example).

H.R. 4884 provides for the failure of a covered bond issuer. If default occurs prior to or without the appointment of the FDIC as conservator or receiver of the issuing institution, then the cover pool assets were to be separated into a separate estate. If the FDIC were appointed the conservator or receiver, the FDIC would have had the right for 180 days to transfer the cover pool and covered bond obligations to another covered bond issuer. If no transfer occurred or the FDIC failed to institute timely cure of a default, then a separate estate would have been created for the affected covered bond programs.

H.R. 5823: United States Covered Bonds Act of 2010

H.R. 5823 would have established a statutory framework for covered bonds similar to that proposed in H.R. 4884. It defined a covered bond in statute, designated a regulator for a covered bond program, created a framework that met the ECBC's definition of a statutory covered bond program, and detailed how covered bonds would be treated should an issuing institution be subjected to an FDIC conservatorship or receivership. It required registration and regulation of covered bonds, with an assessment on the industry to cover the cost of regulation. Covered bonds issued by approved programs would have been subject to overcollateralization and asset coverage requirements.

There were some differences between H.R. 4884 and H.R. 5823. The language of H.R. 5823 as introduced would have switched the covered bond program regulator from the Treasury to the OCC (this was further amended in markup to be the issuer's primary financial regulator, as discussed below). ABSs would no longer have been listed as eligible assets for the cover pools. H.R. 5823 specified that covered bonds are "a security issued or guaranteed by a bank," not asset backed securities. This distinguished covered bonds from securitization. Each covered bond issuance was to specify an independent asset monitor for the cover pool, instead of allowing reports to the covered bond regulator to serve as independent asset monitoring. H.R. 5823 also included a study by the Federal Reserve on whether Fed banks should be empowered to make advances to a covered bond estate resulting from the failure of an institution in conservatorship or receivership. The study would have considered only advances provided solely for the purpose of providing liquidity in the case of timing mismatches among the assets and the liabilities of the estate.

H.R. 5823 was marked up by the House Financial Services Committee on July 29, 2010. After amendments by Representatives Kanjorski, Bean, and

Garrett, the committee reported the bill favorably to the House. The amendments designated each issuer's primary federal financial regulator as the regulator for its covered bonds programs. Rulemaking for covered bonds were to be conducted jointly by the OCC, the Federal Reserve, the FDIC, and the SEC. However, the agencies would have been given a time limit to issue joint rules, after which rulemaking authority would have been given to the Treasury. The covered bond regulator for an institution would have had to consult with the FDIC and confirm that the program would not materially increase the risk of losses or actual losses to the deposit insurance fund prior to approving an institution's covered bonds program.

Several other technical amendments were in the July 29 markup. The amendments eliminated reference to home equity loans, auto loans, student loans, and credit card loans from the definition of "eligible asset" in Section 2 (7), although the provision for the covered bond regulator to add "any other asset class" to the definition of "eligible asset class" by rule in Section 2 (8)(E) was not eliminated. Subsidiaries of bank holding companies and savings and loan holding companies were added to the definition of "eligible issuers." Fees levied by the covered bond regulator on issuers of covered bonds to cover the costs of regulation shall not be construed as government funds or appropriated monies.

End Notes

[1] International Monetary Fund (IMF), *Global Financial Stability Report*, "Chapter 2: Restarting Securitization Markets," October 2009, available at
http://www.imf.org/external/pubs/ft/gfsr/2009/02/pdf/chap2.pdf.

[2] "Covered Bonds in the EU Financial System," European Central Bank, December 2008, p. 6, available at http://www.ecb.int/pub/pdf/other/coverbonds intheeufinancialsystem 200812en_en.pdf.

[3] "Covered Bond Primer for the Uninitiated," Sabine Winkler and Alexander Batchvarov, Bank of America Merrill Lynch, January 22, 2010, at http://ihfp.wharton.upenn.edu/Main%20 Course%20Readings%5CModule%20V%20-%20Types%20of%20Funding%20Models %5 CMortgage%20Bond%20Funding/B-BOA,%20ML%20-%20Covered%20Bond%20Primer.pdf.

[4] "FDIC Policy Statement on Covered Bonds," FIL 73-2008, FDIC, August 4, 2008, available at http://www.fdic.gov/ news/news/financial/2008/fil08073.html.

[5] IMF, *Global Financial Stability Report*, "Chapter 2: Restarting Securitization Markets," October 2009, available at http://www.imf.org/external/pubs/ft/gfsr/2009/02/pdf/chap2.pdf.

[6] "Testimony of Patricia McCoy Before the Senate Committee on Banking, Housing, and Urban Affairs," October 7, 2009, available at http://banking.senate.gov/public

/index.cfm?FuseAction=Files.View&FileStore_id=02242b1f-27e9-4aa0-ae0f-3a1c0 eacc7e6.

[7] "Written testimony of Wesley Phoa," House Committee on Financial Services, December 15, 2009, available at http://www.house.gov/apps/list/hearing/financialsvcs_dem/phoa.pdf.

[8] IMF, *Global Financial Stability Report*, "Chapter 2: Restarting Securitization Markets," October 2009, available at http://www.imf.org/external/pubs/ft/gfsr/2009/02/pdf/chap2.pdf.

[9] "Asset Securitization," Comptrollers Handbook, OCC, 1997, available at http://www.occ.treas.gov/handbook/ assetsec.pdf.

[10] Regulated banks are subject to a number of regulatory and risk-based capital requirements. Mortgage loans and other risky lending assets that are held on bank balance sheets require capital in relation to their risk. Typically, a bank that sells or securitizes a loan no longer has to hold its associated risk-based capital for that asset.

[11] "Regulatory Capital Standards: Final Rule Amending the Risk-Based Capital Rules to Reflect the Issuance of FAS 166 and FAS 167," Financial Institution Letter FIL 3-2010, FDIC, January 21, 2010, available at http://www.fdic.gov/ news/news/financial/ 2010/fil10003.html.

[12] The term duration is often used to refer to a more precise measure of risks associated with timing on a financial institution's balance sheet.

[13] "Optimal Securitization with Moral Hazard," Barney Hartman-Glasery, Tomasz Piskorskiz, and Alexei Tchistyix, January 19, 2010, working paper available at http://faculty.haas.berkeley.edu/bhglaser/optimal_securitization.pdf.

[14] "The Federal Home Loan Bank System: The Lender of Next to Last Resort," Adam Ashcraft, Morten Bech, and Scott Frame, Federal Reserve Bank of New York Staff Reports, No. 357, November 2008, available at http://www.ny.frb.org/research/staff_reports/sr357.pdf.

[15] Private-label securitizations refer to mortgage-backed securities that are issued by firms other than the government-sponsored enterprises, Fannie Mae and Freddie Mac. Monthly private label mortgage securitizations approached zero, according to statistics from the Securities Industry and Financial Markets Association (SIFMA), available at http://www.sifma.org/uploadedFiles/Research/Statistics/SIFMA_USMortgageRelatedIssuan ce.pdf.

[16] "Remarks by Secretary Henry M. Paulson Jr. on Recommendations from the President's Working Group on Financial Markets," Press Release, U.S. Department of Treasury, March 13, 2008, available at http://www.treas.gov/ press/releases/hp1102.htm.

[17] "Treasury Releases Best Practices to Encourage Additional Form of Mortgage Finance," Press Release, U.S. Department of Treasury, July 28, 2008, available at http://www.treas.gov/press/releases/hp1102.htm.

[18] "Best Practices for Residential Covered Bonds", U.S. Department of Treasury, July 2008, available at http://www.treas.gov/press/releases/reports/USCoveredBondBestPractices.pdf.

[19] "FDIC Policy Statement on Covered Bonds," Federal Deposit Insurance Corporation, August 4, 2008, available at http://www.fdic.gov/news/news/financial

[20] "Covered Bond Policy Statement," Federal Register, Vol. 73, No. 145, July 28, 2008.

[21] "Treasury, Federal Reserve and the FDIC Provide Assistance to Bank of America," press release, FDIC, January 16, 2009, available at http://www.fdic.gov/news/news/ press/2009/pr09004.html.

[22] Alison Vekshin, "FDIC Adding Covered Bonds to Liquidity Guarantee Program," Bloomberg News, January 16, 2009, available at http://www.bloomberg.com/apps/news?pid =20601087&sid=acuw6oiWXLvw&refer=home.

[23] Rebecca Christie, "FDIC Won't Extend Bank-Debt Guarantee Plan," *Boston Globe*, May 16, 2009, available at http://www.boston.com/business/articles/2009/05/16/fdic_ wont_extend_ bank_debt_guarantee_plan.

[24] European Covered Bond Council, "ECBC Covered Bond Statistics for 2008," available at http://www.hypo.org/ DocShareNoFrame/docs/2/KBMNBDGCAANJIAHPHIOKEAPOPDBG9DBYA1TE4Q/E MF/Docs/DLS/2009- 00135.pdf.

[25] For a comparative analysis of legal-based and structured bonds, see European Central Bank, "Covered Bonds in the EU Financial System," December 2008, available at http://www.ecb.int/pub/pdf/other/ coverbondsintheeufinancialsystem200812en_en.pdf.

[26] The legislative text of both Article 22(4) of UCITS and the CRD are available at http://ecbc.hypo.org/content/ default.asp?PageID=317.

[27] "Covered Bonds in the EU Financial System," European Central Bank, December 2008, available at http://www.ecb.int/pub/pdf/other/coverbondsintheeufinancial system 200812en_en.pdf.

[28] European Central Bank, "Purchase Programme for Covered Bonds," press release, June 4, 2009, available at http://www.ecb.int/press/pr/date/2009/html/pr090604_1.en.html.

[29] European Central Bank, "Financial Stability Review, June 2010, p. 80, available at http://www.ecb.int/pub/pdf/other/ financialstabilityreview201006en.pdf?c66ac55577ca1ed83cd72b4d92aa17ec.

[30] During the 110th Congress, Congressman Garrett introduced a bill with identical legislative text; the Equal Treatment for Covered Bonds Act of 2008, H.R. 6659.

In: Covered Bonds: Features and Proposals ISBN: 978-1-61470-118-7
Editors: Wei Zhao and Chan Li © 2011 Nova Science Publishers, Inc.

Chapter 2

TESTIMONY OF SCOTT A. STENGEL, BEFORE THE U.S. HOUSE SUBCOMMITTEE ON CAPITAL MARKETS AND GOVERNMENT SPONSORED ENTERPRISES, HEARING ON "LEGISLATIVE PROPOSALS TO CREATE A COVERED BOND MARKET IN THE UNITED STATES"[*]

Chairman Garrett, Ranking Member Waters, and Members of the Subcommittee, I am grateful for your invitation to testify today on the crucial role that U.S. covered bonds can play in stabilizing our financial system and contributing to our economic recovery.

I am a partner in the Washington, D.C., office of King & Spalding LLP and a member of the Steering Committee for the U.S. Covered Bond Council (the Council). The Council is a collaborative forum comprised of investors, issuers, dealers, and other participants in the covered-bond market, and we strive to develop policies and practices that harmonize the views of these different constituencies and that promote a vibrant market for U.S. covered bonds.[1]

---

[*] This is an edited, reformatted and augmented version of testimony given by Scott A. Stengel, before the U.S. House Subcommittee on Capital Markets and Government Sponsored Enterprises, Hearing on "Legislative Proposals to Create a Covered Bond Market in the United States" on March 11, 2011.

When I last testified before the House Financial Services Committee in December 2009 on the need for U.S. covered bonds, policymakers faced an economic recovery that was slow and uneven. Fifteen months later, the environment is little changed. The percentage of unemployed or underemployed Americans has declined less than half a point from 17.1% to 16.7%. Despite over 1 million distressed home sales in 2010 and an increase in the distressed-sale discount from 30% to 37%, the percentage of negative-equity households has held steady at approximately 23%. The S&P/Case-Shiller National Home Price Index is down 4.1% since the fourth quarter of 2009, which is the lowest annual growth rate since the third quarter of 2009 when prices were falling at an annual rate of 8.6%. The delinquency rate on loans backing commercial mortgage-backed securities has increased to a record 9.39%, even though more loans were modified in 2010 than in the prior two years combined. State tax collections, adjusted for inflation, are down 12% from pre-recession levels, and for fiscal year 2012, 45 States and the District of Columbia are projecting budget shortfalls.

In the Council's view, sustained economic growth begins with a stable financial system. While the Dodd-Frank Act has supplied some important structural elements, there remains a considerable need for long-term and cost-effective funding that is sourced from diverse parts of the private-sector capital markets and that can be translated into meaningful credit for households, small businesses, and the public sector.

We believe that U.S. covered bonds are an untapped but proven resource that could be invaluable in meeting this need. The recent financial crisis has confirmed once again that nonlinearities and information constraints preclude reliable economic forecasts and that systemic risk is best mitigated by enabling markets to flex and market participants to pivot in short order. This, in turn, requires that financial intermediaries have more rather than fewer tools at their disposal to maintain a constant flow of credit through the economy, and essential among these tools are covered bonds.

We also believe that the time for U.S. covered bonds is now. While the balance sheets of financial institutions cannot replace the multi-trillion dollar securitization market, covered bonds can bridge funding gaps in the short term and can supply a much needed source of complementary liquidity in the long term. Similarly, while covered bonds are no panacea for the difficult policy issues that have been raised in the context of GSE reform, a robust covered-bond market would immediately attract private capital without need of a federal subsidy and would ultimately contribute to a more stable system of mortgage finance. With the success of a fragile economic recovery hanging in the balance, we simply cannot afford to wait any longer.

THE BENEFITS OF A U.S. COVERED-BOND MARKET

Much has been written about U.S. covered bonds in the last two years, and because not all of the commentary has been entirely accurate, I want to take just a moment to describe this financial tool. At its core, a covered bond is simply a form of high-grade senior debt that is issued by a regulated financial institution and that is secured – or "covered" – by a dynamic cover pool of financial assets which is continually replenished. What distinguishes covered bonds from other secured debt is a legislatively or sometimes contractually prescribed process for managing (rather than immediately liquidating) the cover pool upon the issuer's default or insolvency and continuing scheduled (rather than accelerated) payments on the covered bonds. Over the course of this product's 240-year history, cover pools have included residential mortgage loans, commercial mortgage loans, agricultural loans, ship loans, and public-sector loans, and in the Council's view, loans for small businesses, students, automobile owners and lessors, and consumers using credit or charge cards also are appropriate.

Covered bonds are an effective vehicle for infusing long-term liquidity into the financial system. With maturities that typically range from 2 to 10 years and that can extend out to 15 years or more, they provide a natural complement to the short- and medium-term funding that is available through the Federal Home Loan Banks (the FHLBs) and the securitization and repo markets. This kind of stable liquidity allows financial companies to turn around and provide long-term credit to consumers, small businesses, and governments without being vulnerable to sudden changes in interest rates or investor confidence. In addition, by using covered bonds to more closely match the maturities of their assets and liabilities, financial institutions are able to reduce refinancing risks that can have a destabilizing influence on the banking system more broadly.

Covered bonds also represent a cost-efficient form of on-balance-sheet financing for financial institutions that, in turn, can reduce the cost of credit for families, small businesses, and the public sector. The importance of this cost efficiency cannot be overstated. Recent accounting changes and increased regulatory capital requirements, as well as continued challenges in the securitization market, have made lending far more expensive. Spreads on long-term unsecured debt, moreover, are substantially wider than the short-term rates that have been pushed down to historically low levels by recent government initiatives, and these long-term rates could move even higher as the federal government exits those initiatives and competes for funding to finance its own budget deficits.

Another benefit of covered bonds is their separate and distinct investor base. These investors are providing liquidity that would not otherwise be made available through the unsecured-debt or securitization markets, and as a result, covered bonds enable financial institutions to add another source of funding rather than merely cannibalize their existing sources. Such diversification, not only in the kind but in the supply of liquidity, is crucial to reducing systemic risk and securing the financial system. With a growing shortage of fixed-income securities of the kind that appeal to rates investors, moreover, covered bonds are attracting as much interest as ever.

Equally important, covered bonds deliver funding from the private-sector capital markets without any reliance on U.S. taxpayers for support. The recent crisis is a stark reminder of how dependent some parts of the financial system have become on government intervention. That kind of intervention not only exposes the taxpayers to risk but also can create significant market dislocations if investors are not incented at the same time to direct their capital to unsubsidized investments. Covered bonds, which have demonstrated resilience even in distressed market conditions, can serve as an important bridge from an economy that is limping along on government support to one that is able to stand and thrive on its own.

Two other features of covered bonds bear mention. First, in contrast to securitization, a financial company issuing covered bonds continues to own the assets in the cover pool that are pledged as security. This creates 100% "skin in the game," and as a result, incentives relating to underwriting, asset performance, and loan modifications are strongly aligned. Second, the success of covered bonds is attributable in no small measure to their high degree of transparency and uniformity. As one of the most straightforward of financial products, covered bonds are a model of safe and sound banking practices.

With covered bonds supplying long-term and cost-efficient liquidity from a separate private-sector investor base, the Council believes that credit will more effectively flow to households, small businesses, and State and local governments. Because covered bonds are ultimately constrained by the balance sheets of issuers, however, they cannot be called a silver bullet, and action still needs to be taken to resuscitate securitization and other parts of the financial markets. But, like some of the measures in the Dodd-Frank Act,

THE NEED FOR A LEGISLATIVE FRAMEWORK

To function successfully, a U.S. covered-bond market must be deep and highly liquid. Covered bonds are viewed as a conservative and defensive investment, and just as with any other high-grade instrument, investors expect active bids, offers, and trades. Sporadic issuances, one - off transactions, cumbersome trading, and shallow supply and demand are incompatible with covered bonds.

This need for a deep and liquid covered-bond market was recognized by the Treasury Department (the Treasury) and the Federal Deposit Insurance Corporation (the FDIC) in 2008 when they collaborated to issue, respectively, Best Practices for Residential Covered Bonds and a Final Covered Bond Policy Statement. Regulators and market participants alike hoped that, in the absence of a legislative framework, these regulatory initiatives might serve as an adequate substitute and foster the growth of U.S. covered bonds.

But, during the last three years, it has become apparent that regulatory guidance alone will not suffice.

Covered bonds were originated and developed in Europe under legislative frameworks that require public supervision designed to protect covered bondholders, and this precedent has set market expectations. Today, almost 30 countries across the continent of Europe have adopted national legislation to govern covered bonds. These include Germany, France, the United Kingdom, the Netherlands, Spain, Italy, Russia, Denmark, Ireland, Portugal, the Czech Republic, the Slovak Republic, Austria, Hungary, Slovenia, Switzerland, Luxembourg, Sweden, Finland, Norway, Poland, Latvia, Lithuania, Ukraine, Romania, Bulgaria, Greece, Armenia, and Turkey. Even in Canada, where financial institutions have been able to actively tap the covered-bond market because of more creditor-friendly insolvency laws and the unique nature of their cover pools, a legislative framework is being developed.

Dedicated covered-bond legislation and public supervision, from the perspective of market participants, creates a degree of legal certainty that regulatory initiatives just cannot replicate. This kind of certainty is critical because the nature of covered bonds as a high-grade defensive investment with limited prepayment risk has no room for ambiguity on the rights and remedies available at law, especially in the event of the issuing institution's insolvency.

Investors will not dedicate funds to this market unless the legal regime is unequivocal and the risks can be identified and underwritten.

To provide an example, if a U.S. depository institution were to issue covered bonds and later enter receivership under existing law, the FDIC has expressed the view that three options are available at its discretion: (1) the FDIC could continue to perform on the covered bonds according to their original terms, (2) the FDIC could repudiate the covered bonds or allow a default to occur, make a determination about the fair market value of the cover pool securing them, pay covered bondholders an amount equal to the lesser of that fair market value and the outstanding principal amount of the covered bonds with interest accrued only to the date of its appointment as receiver, and retain the cover pool, or (3) the FDIC could repudiate the covered bonds or allow a default to occur, leave covered bondholders to exercise self-help remedies against the cover pool, and recover from them any proceeds in excess of the outstanding principal amount of the covered bonds with interest accrued only to the date of its appointment as receiver. Any of these three options would be exercised against the backdrop of a temporary automatic stay that would last for 90 days after the FDIC's appointment as receiver or, at best under the Final Covered Bond Policy Statement, 10 business days after an uncured monetary default (though not an uncured nonmonetary default).

In these circumstances, investors face a number of uncertainties: Which of the three options will the FDIC exercise? When will the FDIC make its choice? How will the FDIC calculate the fair market value of the cover pool, and how long will that process take? Will self-help remedies alone suffice, or will the FDIC instead need to be involved in releasing the cover pool? Will the FDIC challenge the method of liquidation used by the trustee for the covered bondholders? What will happen if the FDIC elects to perform for some period of time and then later repudiate, especially if the cover pool has deteriorated in the meantime? Legal uncertainties like these simply do not exist under the legislative frameworks found in Europe.

Equally troubling to investors and other market participants is the fact that this optionality resides with the FDIC, which has a rather clear conflict of interest because of its fiduciary duty to depositors and the deposit-insurance fund. The conflict was recently highlighted by the FDIC's repeated calls for legislation that would force secured creditors like covered bondholders to take a haircut even if their claims are fully collateralized – a development which, to our knowledge, would be unprecedented in the history of credit.[2] Although this proposal was not adopted as part of the Dodd-Frank Act, the FDIC's advocacy was sufficiently vigorous to prompt a wide-ranging study on the subject.[3]

Layered on top of these concerns is the obvious incompatibility of a forced acceleration by the FDIC with the core nature of a covered bond. A *sine qua non* of covered bonds is the use of collections and other proceeds from the cover pool to continue making scheduled payments after the issuer's default or insolvency. If forced acceleration were possible, the instrument would no longer be a covered bond but instead would be just plain-vanilla secured debt. In addition, if the FDIC were to take the position that secured claims of investors are limited to the fair market value of the cover pool at a moment in time rather than to its cash flow value over time, forced acceleration would expose them to losses arising from short-term market volatility and liquidity risks that are not part of the economic bargain in the covered-bond market.

For these reasons, the Council has concluded that a well-functioning market for U.S. covered bonds cannot develop without a legislative framework that stays true to the distinctive features of traditional covered bonds. Anything less would preclude issuing institutions – and ultimately consumers, small businesses, and the public sector – from realizing the cost efficiencies that make covered bonds worthwhile.

We are confident, moreover, that such a framework could be constructed in a way to fully protect the interests of an issuer's other creditors (including, in the case of a bank, the deposit-insurance fund) as well as any conservator, receiver, or bankruptcy trustee. Taking a bank receivership as an example once again, we would support a period of up to 180 days for the FDIC to transfer an affected covered-bond program to another eligible issuer so long as all monetary and nonmonetary obligations were performed during that time.[4] If such a transfer turned out to be impossible or inadvisable and the covered-bond program were moved to a separate estate for administration, we believe that the receivership's equity in that estate should take the form of a residual interest that the FDIC could sell or otherwise monetize immediately for the benefit of other creditors and the deposit-insurance fund. We also could support the holder of that equity interest being afforded consent rights over the selection of any servicer or administrator for the estate.

The absence of a legislative framework for U.S. covered bonds is already coming at a cost. European and other non-U.S. issuers have been taking advantage of favorable laws in their home countries and filling the vacuum. In 2010 alone, over $27 billion in U.S. Dollar covered bonds were targeted to investors in the United States, and over $55 billion more is expected in 2011. With governments in Europe providing the requisite legal certainty for covered

28 Testimony of Scott A. Stengel

bonds issued by their domestic institutions, we fear that the playing field could grow increasingly uneven in the fierce competition among banks for less expensive and more stable sources of funding.

The cost of such an outcome, of course, will be born in the end by families, small businesses, and governments throughout the United States, especially those that are dependent on banks for their liquidity needs. When possible, the higher funding costs will be passed along to them; when not, credit will be denied altogether. Neither result can be described as at all desirable.

SOME MYTHS DISPELLED

Myth – U.S. covered bonds would have an implicit federal guarantee.
Fact – U.S. covered bonds would not be backed, either explicitly or implicitly, by the federal government.

The implicit federal guarantee enjoyed by Fannie Mae, Freddie Mac, and the FHLBs has arisen from an extraordinarily unique set of components:

- Each GSE has been federally chartered with a targeted public-policy purpose.[5]
- The U.S. Treasury has been authorized to extend credit to each GSE.[6]
- Each GSE has been exempted from most State and local income taxes.[7]
- Each GSE's debt securities and mortgage-backed securities have been made eligible for open-market purchases by the Federal Reserve Banks,[8] for deposits of public funds,[9] and for investments by fiduciaries.[10]
- Each GSE's debt securities and mortgage-backed securities have been exempted from investment limits that are otherwise imposed on banks, savings associations, and credit unions.[11]
- Each GSE has been entitled to use any Federal Reserve Bank as its depository, custodian, and fiscal agent.[12]

Under the legislative framework that the Council has proposed, no issuer of U.S. covered bonds could lay claim to any status or preference that even remotely resembles those afforded to the GSEs. For example, to the extent that any misguided inference could be drawn from a covered-bond estate inheriting an insolvent issuer's access to liquidity from the Federal Reserve Banks, we have proposed that legislation expressly provide that (1) no advance can be made by a Federal Reserve Bank for the purpose, or with the expectation, of absorbing credit losses on the estate's cover pool, (2) any advance must have a maturity that is consistent with an advance for liquidity only, (3) repayment of any advance must constitute a superpriority claim against the estate that is secured by a superpriority lien on the cover pool, and (4) any Federal Reserve Bank making an advance must promptly report to Congress on the circumstances giving rise to the advance, the terms of the advance, the nature of the cover pool securing the advance, and the basis for concluding that credit losses on the cover pool will not be absorbed by the Federal Reserve Bank.

Some have suggested that the mere existence of a single covered-bond regulator could imply that covered bonds are backed to some degree by the U.S. government. This, in our view, is a questionable proposition. After all, a single regulator – the Comptroller of the Currency (the OCC) – supervises all national banks, but no one could seriously argue that the OCC is an implied-in-fact guarantor of their obligations. Similarly, the Securities and Exchange Commission regulates all non-exempt offers and sales of securities but certainly could not be perceived as insuring investors against any loss.

Our reservation about multiple covered-bond regulators, as some have proposed, is rooted in a conviction that market fragmentation would likely doom U.S. covered bonds from the outset. We cannot envision a deep and liquid market developing if national banks, State member banks, State nonmember banks, bank holding companies, and other covered-bond issuers are operating under different regulatory frameworks. At a minimum, therefore, we recommend that the Secretary of the Treasury be directed to promulgate a single set of regulations for all covered-bond issuers and that each of the individual prudential regulators be tasked with implementing them for the issuers under their primary supervision. This, in our view, would not be ideal but at least would allow for the kind of uniform legal regime that will be critical to developing a vibrant market for U.S. covered bonds.

We also are aware of the FDIC's assertion that the legislative framework proposed by the Council would give covered bondholders "a super-priority in receivership" and would result in their claims being "essentially back-stopped by the FDIC."[13] These statements, however, were not substantiated and, in our view, reflect a fundamental misunderstanding of the proposal and existing law.

A superpriority claim or a superpriority lien, in the context of an insolvency proceeding, is one that has been elevated to a level of priority

30   Testimony of Scott A. Stengel

higher than that otherwise afforded by applicable law to other claims or liens (including administrative claims or liens).[14]

Nothing in our proposed legislative framework, including the treatment of any claim or lien of a covered bondholder, would change the priority scheme in a conservatorship or receivership of the issuing institution. Both before and after the insolvency proceeding, investors would benefit from a first-priority lien on the issuer's cover pool to secure their claims under the covered bonds – just like any other secured creditor – and at no time would they be entitled to a lien (superpriority or otherwise) on any of the issuer's other assets. In addition, to the extent that the cover pool proves insufficient to satisfy their claims in full, covered bondholders would fall in line alongside all other general unsecured creditors without any enhanced priority or preference of any kind. This treatment stands in stark contrast, for example, to the superpriority claims and liens that can arise in connection with post-insolvency financing arrangements[15] and to the springing priority of an FHLB's "super lien" on all of a member institution's property.[16]

What our legislative proposal would affect is the FDIC's power to compel an acceleration of the covered bonds and to pay only "actual direct compensatory damages . . . determined as of the date of the appointment of the conservator or receiver."[17] Because a *sine qua non* of covered bonds is their limited risk of prepayment, they instead would remain outstanding according to their original terms so long as collections and other proceeds from the cover pool could continue to fund all scheduled payments.

This, however, hardly creates a backstop by the FDIC. To the contrary, our proposal is a more modest iteration of the framework that currently exists for qualified financial contracts (QFCs) under the Federal Deposit Insurance Act (the FDIA). One notable similarity between them is full restitution, at least to the extent of the posted collateral (including any overcollateralization), for damages that result from reinvestment risk. In the context of QFCs, this is picked up by the counterparty's right under the FDIA to "normal and reasonable costs of cover or other reasonable measures of damages utilized in the industries for such contract and agreement claims."[18] Another similarity is found in carefully drawn limits on the FDIC's ability to repudiate or assign contracts or collateral.[19] But, unlike covered bondholders in our proposed framework, a QFC counterparty is entitled to even more, including (1) a unilateral right to terminate, liquidate, or accelerate the QFC and to exercise remedies and rights of setoff under the QFC and against any related collateral,[20] (2) an ability, after the business day following the date of the FDIC's appointment as receiver, to enforce ordinarily nonbinding contractual provisions that are triggered solely by the institution's insolvency or receivership (*ipso facto* clauses),[21] and (3) immunity from all avoidance actions except for those grounded in an actual intent to defraud.[22]

We may be able to support a legislative framework for U.S. covered bonds that is modeled on these QFC provisions, if the use of existing precedent would assuage even misplaced concerns.

Myth – U.S. covered bonds would benefit only the largest banks.
Fact – The U.S. covered-bond market would be available to regional and community banks under the proposed legislative framework.

Covered bonds are a conservative and defensive investment that appeals to investors only if the secondary market is sufficiently deep and liquid to generate active bids, offers, and trades. As a result, each series of covered bonds is typically sized at no less than $500 million.

To ensure that regional and community banks are able to access such a market on competitive terms, we have proposed that pooled issuances be permitted. Under this arrangement, several institutions would issue more modestly sized series of covered bonds to a statutory trust or other separate entity that they have collectively sponsored. This entity then would populate a cover pool with the multiple series that have been acquired and issue into the market a single series of covered bonds backed by all of them together.

In this way, for example, each of ten community banks could establish its own separate covered-bond program comprised of the commercial-mortgage loans on its balance sheet and issue $50 million of related covered bonds to a jointly sponsored trust. All ten of these separate $50 million series of covered bonds then would fill a cover pool established by the trust, and a single $500 million series of covered bonds backed by the entire cover pool would be issued by the trust to investors.

We believe that this approach, which has been used successfully in Europe, would open the U.S. covered-bond market to regional and community banks in a meaningful way. We also believe that the cost-effective, long-term funding that covered bonds can supply would be especially valuable to small- and middle-market institutions that historically have been limited to fewer and less diverse sources of liquidity.

Myth – U.S. covered bonds would merely replace FHLB advances and therefore result in a reallocation of, and not an increase in, funding for financial institutions.

Fact – U.S. covered bonds would constitute an additive source of liquidity for financial institutions and, as a result, would facilitate increased lending.

Each individual decision to lend is a function of return on capital, business strategy, and risk management.

Covered bonds enable financial institutions (1) to lower the cost of funding, which increases the return on capital, (2) to augment rather than cannibalize their funding sources, which provides the fuel for business lines to innovate and boost lending, and (3) to better match assets and liabilities, which reduces the risk of providing longer-term closed-end loans (like residential mortgage loans) and revolving lines of credit (like credit-card loans).

As a result, we must respectfully disagree with any suggestion that covered bonds will not contribute to increased lending. That, in our view, is not supported by the microeconomic incentives that drive the business of banking or by any empirical data.

We also must take issue with any suggestion that covered bonds are similar or equivalent to advances from the FHLBs. First, covered bonds will fund a much broader range of asset classes than the FHLBs typically accept in the normal course of business. Second, covered bonds will supply fixed-rate liquidity with maturities that the FHLBs generally do not offer to their member institutions. For these reasons, we envision covered bonds as a private-sector complement, rather than as a substitute, for federally subsidized FHLB advances.

All of this being said, we can foresee financial institutions reallocating a modest portion of their short-and medium-term funding away from existing sources and toward a U.S. covered-bond market that is deep and liquid. But this, in our view, is the very macroeconomic objective that policymakers are seeking to achieve. The liquidity crisis that began in late 2008 was exacerbated in no small part by an overreliance on volatile short-term borrowings to fund longterm assets. Covered bonds will provide financial institutions with a cost-effective source of fixed-rate funding much farther out on the maturity curve than is currently feasible, which will lessen systemic risk in the broader financial markets and will bolster risk-management frameworks inside individual institutions.

PROPOSAL FOR A LEGISLATIVE FRAMEWORK

The Council fully supports the kind of comprehensive covered-bond legislation that Chairman Garrett and Representative Maloney have proposed in the United States Covered Bond Act of 2011 (H.R. 940).

In particular, the Council endorses the following elements of a legislative framework for U.S. covered bonds:

- *Public Supervision by a Covered Bond Regulator* – The public supervision of covered-bond programs by a federal regulator, whose mission is the protection of covered bondholders, is central to any legislative framework. In the European Union, this feature is enshrined in Article 52(4) of the Directive on Undertakings for Collective Investment in Transferable Securities (the UCITS Directive).[23] Compliance with Article 52(4) is what has given covered bonds their unique status in Europe, including privileged risk weighting under the EU's Capital Requirements Directive and preferential treatment by the European Central Bank in Eurosystem credit operations.

We therefore support a framework that includes the following: The Secretary of the Treasury, the Comptroller of the Currency, or another U.S. government agency – excluding the FDIC because of its conflict of interest – would be appointed as the Covered Bond Regulator, which would have as its mission the protection of covered bondholders. The Covered Bond Regulator, in consultation with other applicable primary federal regulators, would ensure compliance with legislative requirements and would establish additional regulatory requirements that are tailored to the different kinds of covered-bond programs. Covered bonds would fall under the legislative framework only if issued under a covered-bond program that has been approved by the Covered Bond Regulator in consultation with the issuer's primary federal regulator. The Covered Bond Regulator would maintain a public registry of approved covered-bond programs.[24]

- *Eligible Issuers* – Issuances by regulated financial institutions is another fundamental element of covered bonds that is also recognized in the UCITS Directive. In order to afford competitive market access to regional and community banks, however, pooled issuances by entities that have been sponsored by one or more regulated institutions should be permitted as well.

We therefore support a framework that includes the following: Eligible issuers of covered bonds would be comprised of (1) depository institutions, domestic branches or agencies of foreign banks, and their subsidiaries, (2) bank holding companies, savings and loan holding companies, and their subsidiaries, (3) nonbank financial companies and their subsidiaries if approved by the Covered Bond Regulator and other applicable primary federal regulators, and (4) issuing entities that are sponsored by one or more eligible issuers for the sole purpose of issuing covered bonds on a pooled basis.

- *Covered Bonds* – To ensure that covered bonds retain their essential attributes as the market evolves, we support a framework that includes the following: A covered bond would be defined as a recourse debt obligation of an eligible issuer that (1) has an original term to maturity of not less than one year, (2) is secured by a perfected security interest in a cover pool that is owned directly or indirectly by the issuer, (3) is issued under a covered-bond program that has been approved by the Covered Bond Regulator, (4) is identified in a register of covered bonds that is maintained by the Covered Bond Regulator, and (5) is not a deposit.
- *Cover Pool* – One other indispensable feature of covered bonds is a cover pool that contains performing assets and that is replenished and kept sufficient at all times to fully secure the claims of covered bondholders. This too receives specific mention in the UCITS Directive.

We therefore support a framework that includes the following: The cover pool would be defined as a dynamic pool of assets that is comprised of (1) one or more eligible assets from a single eligible asset class, (2) substitute assets (such as cash and cash equivalents) without limitation, and (3) ancillary assets (such as swaps, credit enhancement, and liquidity arrangements) without limitation. No cover pool would include eligible assets from more than one eligible asset class. A loan would not qualify as an eligible asset while delinquent for more than 60 consecutive days, and a security would not qualify as an eligible asset while not of the requisite credit quality.

- *Eligible Asset Classes* – The real benefit of covered bonds is long-term and cost-effective funding from the private sector that can be converted into meaningful credit for families, small businesses, and State and local governments throughout the United States.

We therefore support a framework that includes the following eligible asset classes: (1) residential mortgage asset class, (2) home equity asset class, (3) commercial mortgage (including multi-family) asset class, (4) public sector asset class, (5) auto asset class, (6) student loan asset class, (7) credit or charge card asset class, (8) small business asset class, and (9) other asset classes designated by the Covered Bond Regulator in consultation with other applicable primary federal regulators.

- *Overcollateralization, Asset-Coverage Test, and Independent Asset Monitor* – Full transparency, independent monitoring, and regular reporting must be among the hallmarks of U.S. covered bonds.

We therefore support a framework that includes the following: The Covered Bond Regulator would establish minimum overcollateralization requirements for covered bonds backed by each of the eligible asset classes based on credit, collection, and interest-rate risks but not liquidity risks. Each cover pool would be required at all times to satisfy an asset-coverage test, which would measure whether the eligible assets and the substitute assets in the cover pool satisfy the minimum overcollateralization requirements. Each issuer would be required to perform the asset-coverage test monthly on each of its cover pools and to report the results to covered bondholders and applicable regulators. Each issuer also would be obligated to appoint the indenture trustee for its covered bonds or another unaffiliated entity as an independent asset monitor, which would periodically verify the results of the asset-coverage test and provide reports to covered bondholders and applicable regulators.

- *Separate Resolution Process for Covered-Bond Programs* – Hand in hand with public supervision is legal certainty on the resolution of a cover pool if the issuer were to default or become insolvent. A dedicated process must exist that provides a clear roadmap for investors, that avoids the waste inherent in a forced liquidation of collateral, and that allows the cover pool to be managed and its value maximized.

Central to this resolution process is the creation of a separate estate – like the ones created under the Bankruptcy Code – for any covered-bond program whose issuer has defaulted or become insolvent. To ensure that timing mismatches among the assets and liabilities of the estate do not unnecessarily erode the cover pool's value or cause a premature default, both private-sector counterparties and the Federal Reserve Banks should be authorized to make advances to the estate on a superpriority basis for liquidity purposes only. Importantly, however, advances by a Federal Reserve Bank should be prohibited if U.S. taxpayers could be exposed to any credit risk whatsoever.

Special rules also are appropriate should the FDIC be appointed as conservator or receiver for an issuer before any default occurs on its covered bonds. All interested parties would benefit if the FDIC were able to transfer the entire covered-bond program to another eligible issuer, much like Washington Mutual's program was conveyed to JPMorgan Chase. As a result, the FDIC should be afforded a reasonable period of time (not to exceed 180 days) to effect such a transfer before a separate estate is created.

In addition, neither an issuer that has defaulted nor its creditors in the case of insolvency should forfeit the value of surplus collateral in the cover pool. To enable this value to be realized promptly by the issuer and its creditors (including the FDIC and the deposit-insurance fund) without disrupting the separate resolution process, a residual interest should be created in the form of an exempted security that can be sold or otherwise monetized immediately. Such an approach should satisfy all constituencies – covered bondholders will be able to rely on the separate, orderly resolution process for their cover pool, and the issuer and its creditors (including the FDIC and the deposit-insurance fund) will not have to wait for that process to conclude before turning any surplus into cash.

We therefore support a framework that includes the following: If covered bonds default before the issuer enters conservatorship, receivership, liquidation, or bankruptcy, a separate estate would be created that is comprised of the applicable cover pool and that assumes liability for the covered bonds and related obligations. Deficiency claims against the issuer would be preserved, and the issuer would receive a residual interest that represents the right to any surplus from the cover pool. The issuer would be obligated to release applicable books, records, and files and, at the election of the Covered Bond Regulator, to continue servicing the cover pool for 120 days.

If the FDIC were appointed as conservator or receiver for an issuer before a default on its covered bonds results in the creation of an estate, the FDIC would have an exclusive right for up to 180 days to transfer the covered-bond program to another eligible issuer. The FDIC as conservator or receiver would be required during this time to perform all monetary and nonmonetary obligations of the issuer under the covered-bond program.

If another conservator, receiver, liquidator, or bankruptcy trustee were appointed for an issuer before a default on its covered bonds results in the creation of an estate or if the FDIC as conservator or receiver did not transfer a covered-bond program to another eligible issuer within the allowed time, a separate estate would be created that is comprised of the applicable cover pool and that assumes liability for the covered bonds and related obligations. The conservator, receiver, liquidating agent, or bankruptcy court would be required to estimate and allow any contingent deficiency claim against the issuer. The conservator, receiver, liquidating agent, or bankruptcy trustee would receive a residual interest that represents the right to any surplus from the cover pool. The conservator, receiver, liquidating agent, or bankruptcy trustee would be obligated to release applicable books, records, and files and, at the election of the Covered Bond Regulator, to continue servicing the cover pool for 120 days.

The Covered Bond Regulator would act as or appoint the trustee of the estate and would be required to appoint and supervise a servicer or administrator for the cover pool. The servicer or administrator would be obligated to collect, realize on, and otherwise manage the cover pool and to invest and use the proceeds and funds received to make required payments on the covered bonds and satisfy other liabilities of the estate. The estate would be authorized to borrow or otherwise procure funds, including from the Federal Reserve Banks. Other than to compel the release of funds that are available and required to be distributed, no court would be able to restrain or affect the resolution of the estate except at the request of the Covered Bond Regulator.

- *Securities Law Provisions* – With covered-bond programs subject to rigorous public supervision, investors will be well protected. As a result, an expansion of existing securities-law exemptions may be appropriate. Regardless, because legal certainty for covered bonds is paramount, we support a framework that includes at least the following: Existing exemptions for securities issued or guaranteed by a bank would apply equally to covered bonds issued or guaranteed by a bank. Each estate would be exempt from all securities laws but would succeed to any requirement of the issuer to file applicable periodic reports. Each residual interest would be exempt from all securities laws.

- *Miscellaneous Provisions* – We also support a framework that includes the following conforming changes to other applicable law: The Secondary Mortgage Market Enhancement Act of 1984 would be expanded to encompass covered bonds. Covered bonds that are backed by the residential mortgage asset class, the home equity asset class, or the commercial mortgage asset class would be qualified mortgages for Real Estate Mortgage Investment Conduits (REMICs) and, subject to regulations that may be promulgated by the Secretary of the Treasury, would be treated as real estate assets in the same manner as REMIC regular interests. The estate would not be treated as a taxable entity, and no transfer of assets or liabilities to an estate would be treated as a taxable event. The acquisition of a covered bond would be treated as the acquisition of a security, and not as a lending transaction, for tax purposes. The Secretary of the Treasury would be authorized to promulgate regulations for covered bonds similar to the provisions of Section 346 of the Bankruptcy Code.

In addition to these elements of a legislative framework, the Council also believes that U.S. covered bonds should be afforded favorable regulatory capital treatment like that found in Europe, including in the context of both risk weighting and liquidity buffers.

CONCLUDING REMARKS

On behalf of the Council, I want to thank Chairman Garrett for holding this hearing and for his leadership on U.S. covered bonds. I also want to thank Representative Maloney for cosponsoring, together with Chairman Garrett, the United States Covered Bond Act of 2011 (H.R. 940).

I would be pleased to answer any questions that Members of the Subcommittee may have.

End Notes

[1] The U.S. Covered Bond Council is sponsored by The Securities Industry and Financial Markets Association (SIFMA). SIFMA brings together the shared interests of hundreds of securities

Testimony of Scott A. Stengel ... 39

firms, banks, and asset managers. SIFMA's mission is to develop policies and practices which strengthen financial markets and which encourage capital availability, job creation, and economic growth while building trust and confidence in the financial industry. SIFMA, with offices in New York and Washington, D.C., is the U.S. regional member of the Global Financial Markets Association. For more information, please visit www.sifma.org.

[2] *See, e.g.*, Sheila C. Bair, Chairman, Federal Deposit Insurance Corporation, Statement on Establishing a Framework for Systemic Risk Regulation before the U.S. Senate Committee on Banking, Housing, and Urban Affairs (July 23, 2009); Sheila C. Bair, Chairman, Federal Deposit Insurance Corporation, Statement on Regulatory Perspectives on Financial Regulatory Reform Proposals before the U.S. House Committee on Financial Services (July 24, 2009); Sheila C. Bair, Chairman, Federal Deposit Insurance Corporation, Remarks to the International Institute of Finance (October 4, 2009); Sheila C. Bair, Chairman, Federal Deposit Insurance Corporation, Statement on Systemic Regulation, Prudential Measures, Resolution Authority, and Securitization before the U.S. House Committee on Financial Services (October 29, 2009).

[3] *See* Section 215 of the Dodd-Frank Wall Street Reform and Consumer Protection Act (12 U.S.C. § 5395).

[4] This would be consistent with the FDIC's existing policy on the treatment of secured obligations. *See* Federal Deposit Insurance Corporation, Statement of Policy Regarding Treatment of Security Interests After Appointment of the Federal Deposit Insurance Corporation as Conservator or Receiver (March 23, 1993).

[5] 12 U.S.C. §§ 1716-1717 (Fannie Mae), 1452-1454 (Freddie Mac), and 1423-1430c (FHLBs).

[6] 12 U.S.C. §§ 1719(c) (Fannie Mae), 1455(c) (Freddie Mac), and 1431(i) (FHLBs).

[7] U.S.C. §§ 1723a(c)(2) (Fannie Mae), 1452(e) (Freddie Mac), and 1433 (FHLBs).

[8] 12 U.S.C. § 355(2) and 12 C.F.R. § 201.108(b) (Fannie Mae, Freddie Mac, and FHLBs).

[9] 12 U.S.C. §§ 1723c (Fannie Mae), 1452(g) (Freddie Mac), and 1435 (FHLBs).

[10] 12 U.S.C. §§ 1723c (Fannie Mae), 1452(g) (Freddie Mac), and 1435 (FHLBs); see also 15 U.S.C. § 77r-1(a) (preempting any contrary State law in connection with the securities of Fannie Mae and Freddie Mac).

[11] 12 U.S.C. §§ 24(Seventh), 335, 1464(c)(1), and 1757(7) (Fannie Mae, Freddie Mac, and FHLBs).

[12] 12 U.S.C. §§ 1723a(g) (Fannie Mae), 1452(d) (Freddie Mac), and 1435 (FHLBs).

[13] *See, e.g.*, Sheila C. Bair, Chairman, Federal Deposit Insurance Corporation, *Keynote Address to the "Mortgages and the Future of Housing Finance Symposium"* (Oct. 25, 2010).

[14] *See, e.g.*, 11 U.S.C. § 364(c) and (d) (in a bankruptcy case, authorizing postpetition loans "with priority over any or all administrative expenses" and "secured by a senior or equal lien on property of the estate that is subject to a lien"); 12 U.S.C. § 4617(i)(11) (for a limited-life regulated entity created by the Federal Housing Finance Agency with respect to Fannie Mae, Freddie Mac, or an FHLB, authorizing loans "with priority over any or all of the obligations of the limited-life regulated entity" and "secured by a senior or equal lien on property of the limited-life regulated entity that is subject to a lien (other than mortgages that collateralize the mortgage-backed securities issued or guaranteed by an enterprise)"); 12 U.S.C. § 5390(b)(2) ("In the event that the [FDIC], as receiver for a covered financial company, is unable to obtain unsecured credit for the covered financial company from commercial sources, the Corporation as receiver may obtain credit or incur debt on the part of the covered financial company, which shall have priority over any or all administrative expenses of the receiver under paragraph (1)(A)."); 12 U.S.C. § 5390(h)(16) (for a bridge financial company created by the FDIC with respect to a covered financial company,

authorizing loans "with priority over any or all of the obligations of the bridge financial company" and "secured by a senior or equal lien on property of the bridge financial company that is subject to a lien").

[15] *See* the authorities cited in note 14.

[16] 12 U.S.C. § 1430(e) ("Notwithstanding any other provision of law, any security interest granted to a Federal Home Loan Bank by any member of any Federal Home Loan Bank or any affiliate of any such member shall be entitled to priority over the claims and rights of any party (including any receiver, conservator, trustee, or similar party having rights of a lien creditor) other than claims and rights that – (1) would be entitled to priority under otherwise applicable law; and (2) are held by actual bona fide purchasers for value or by actual secured parties that are secured by actual perfected security interests."); *see also* 12 U.S.C. §§ 1821(d)(5)(D) (precluding the FDIC from disallowing any claim asserted by an FHLB) and 1821(e)(14) (exempting FHLB advances from the FDIC's authority to disallow or repudiate contracts).

[17] 12 U.S.C. § 1821(e)(1) and (3).

[18] 12 U.S.C. § 1821(e)(3)(C).

[19] 12 U.S.C. § 1821(e)(9) and (11).

[20] 12 U.S.C. § 1821(e)(8)(A) and (E).

[21] 12 U.S.C. § 1821(e)(10)(B).

[22] 12 U.S.C. § 1821(e)(8)(C).

[23] Article 52(4) will replace its predecessor, Article 22(4), in July 2011 as part of the recast of EU Directive 85/611 by EU Directive 2009/65 (July 13, 2009).

[24] As noted earlier, we also could support a framework where the Secretary of the Treasury is directed to promulgate a single set of regulations for all covered-bond issuers and where each of the individual prudential regulators is tasked with implementing them for the issuers under its primary supervision.

In: Covered Bonds: Features and Proposals   ISBN: 978-1-61470-118-7
Editors: Wei Zhao and Chan Li   © 2011 Nova Science Publishers, Inc.

Chapter 3

TESTIMONY OF BERT ELY, BEFORE THE U.S. HOUSE SUBCOMMITTEE ON CAPITAL MARKETS AND GOVERNMENT SPONSORED ENTERPRISES, HEARING ON "LEGISLATIVE PROPOSALS TO CREATE A COVERED BOND MARKET IN THE UNITED STATES"[*]

Mr. Chairman Garrett, Ranking Member Waters, and members of the Subcommittee, I very much appreciate the opportunity to testify today about covered bonds and legislation to create the legal framework for a vibrant covered-bond market in the United States, specifically H.R. 940. I will first provide a brief description of covered bonds but focus most of my testimony on why Congress needs to enact a covered-bond statute and the many benefits covered bonds will bring to the United States, and specifically to housing finance. I will close by offering some specific comments on H.R. 940.

By way of background, I am a long-time champion of covered-bond financing, on *a pro bono* basis. I have not received any compensation with regard to my work on covered bonds nor for my testimony today. On December 15, 2009, I testified to the Financial Services Committee about covered bonds.

---

[*] This is an edited, reformatted and augmented version of testimony given by Bert Ely, before the U.S. House Subcommittee on Capital Markets and Government Sponsored Enterprises, Hearing on "Legislative Proposals to Create a Covered Bond Market in the United States" on March 11, 2011.

A Brief Description of Covered Bonds

The covered bond concept is quite simple. Essentially, covered bonds are debt instruments issued by a bank or any other type of financial firm which are secured by assets owned outright by the issuer. The bonds also are a direct liability of the issuer, which provides a second source of repayment should the assets securing the covered bonds be insufficient to provide for repayment. In this regard, covered bonds differ sharply from asset securitization wherein assets are sold to a bankruptcy-remote trust which then issues debt securities of various types and tranches to pay for the purchase of those assets.

The unique feature of covered bonds is the "cover pool," which consists of specifically identified assets directly owned by the covered-bond issuer. These assets collectively secure a set of covered bonds. That is, there are multiple assets securing multiple bonds. This multiplicity differentiates covered bonds from mortgage bonds, where a single asset, such as a large office building, is the sole security for one or more mortgage bonds.

To provide a high level of security for the covered bonds, so that they can earn a very high credit rating, the size of the cover pool must always exceed by some factor the amount of bonds secured by the cover pool. That is, the bonds are overcollateralized. For example, the total assets in the cover pool must at all times at least equal 104% or some other percentage greater than 100% of the face amount or par value of the bonds the cover-pool assets secure.

Further, every asset in the pool must always be performing in accordance with covered-bond regulations and the terms of the bond indenture governing a particular issue of covered bonds. For example, a home mortgage in a cover pool cannot be more than 60 days past-due in its scheduled payments, the loan-to-value (LTV) ratio must be below 80%, and the borrower's FICO credit score must be above 700.

If an asset in the cover pool ceases to perform in the manner prescribed by regulation or in a more restrictive bond indenture, the bond issuer must immediately replace that asset with another eligible asset performing in the prescribed manner. This "evergreening" feature ensures that the covered bonds will always be extremely well secured by high-quality assets, which is absolutely essential to obtaining and maintaining a very high credit rating, usually AAA, for the bonds.

Figure 1 attached to this testimony illustrates a simplified balance sheet of a covered-bond issuer. In particular, it emphasizes the on-balance-sheet nature of both covered bonds and the assets in the cover pool securing those bonds. Assets of the covered-bond issuer would move in and out of the cover pool merely through a change in the issuer's financial records as to whether a specific asset was designated as a cover-pool asset.

There would be no external legal recordation as to whether a particular asset was designated as a cover-pool asset. However, an independent "cover pool monitor" or "asset monitor" would continuously monitor the composition of the cover pool to ensure that the covered-bond issuer was continuously in compliance with all applicable regulations as well as all terms of the bond indenture. Given today's technology, that should be a relatively low-cost and highly reliable auditing process.

Numerous types of credit instruments can be financed with covered bonds. Home mortgages represent the largest class of credit instruments which are candidates for covered-bond financing. Other types of credit instruments which are candidates for covered-bond financing include (1) home equity loans; (2) commercial mortgages, including multifamily residential mortgages; (3) debt issued by municipalities and public authorities; (4) automobiles, trucks, construction equipment, and other moveable forms of equipment; (5) ships and airplanes; (6) student loans; (7) credit-card and charge-card receivables; (8) small business loans; (9) leased equipment; and (10) any other type of credit instrument for which covered-bond financing makes economic sense.

It would not be unreasonable to initially authorize just a few classes of assets as eligible for covered-bond financing — home mortgages, commercial and multi-family mortgages, and debt issued by municipalities and public authorities. Once covered-bond financing was well-established for those asset classes, then covered-bond financing could be authorized for other classes of assets.

The following table, based on Federal Reserve Flow of Funds data', provides some sense of the magnitude of credit instruments which could be funded with covered bonds. While covered bonds will not come close to providing 100% of this funding, even a 10% share would be enormous — over $2 trillion, which begins to approach the size of the well-established European covered-bond market.

Types of credit instruments which potentially could be funded with covered bonds
(dollars in billions)

Home mortgages	$ 9,637
Home equity loans	975
Multifamily residential mortgages	847
Commercial non-residential mortgages	2,356
Farm mortgages	133
Total mortgage debt	13,947
Consumer credit of all types	2,409
Non-mortgage borrowings by non-financial businesses	2,779
Local government debt[2]	1,447
Total debt potentially financeable by covered bonds	$20,582

IMPORTANT ATTRIBUTES OF COVERED BONDS

Covered bonds offer important attributes which are often overlooked or misunderstood, including the following.

Covered Bonds Will Not Be Explicitly or Implicitly Backed by the Federal Government

Contrary to the assertions of some, covered bonds will not be explicitly or implicitly backed by the federal government. Clearly, H.R. 940 does not provide an explicit federal guarantee of covered bonds issued under the provisions of this bill.

Further, no provision in H.R. 940 can reasonably be argued as even suggesting an implicit federal guarantee of covered bonds. There is a widespread, and legitimate, belief among investors that when a GSE bond default threatens, an implicit federal guarantee of that debt, by virtue of the issuer's GSE status, will become explicit, as has been the practical effect of the Fannie Mae and Freddie Mac conservatorships. Covered-bond issuers will not have GSE-like federal charters. Further, federal regulation of covered-bond issuance is no more a government guarantee of covered bonds than is the regulation of securities issuance by the SEC. The thrust of covered-bond regulation is merely to ensure that covered-bonds will be at all times purely private-sector credit instruments of the highest possible credit quality.

The authority the bill grants to the FDIC (Sec.(d)(6)) to assess against all covered-bond issuers any incremental losses the FDIC suffers in protecting insured depositors in a failed covered-bond issuer further undercuts the argument that covered bonds will have any taxpayer backing, which is the effect of any government guarantee. Likewise, any authority the Federal Reserve would be granted to lend against or to purchase covered bonds, as I recommend, can and should be structured statutorily so that such Fed lending or purchasing would not cause any loss to taxpayers; i.e., a reduction in the amount of income the Federal Reserve periodically returns to the Treasury.

COVERED BONDS WILL ENHANCE THE ABILITY OF LENDERS TO OFFER 30-YEAR, FIXED-RATE MORTGAGES

Covered bonds will enable banks to make and hold in portfolio 30-year fixed-rate mortgages because covered bonds can be issued at medium and long-term maturities at a fixed-rate of interest. Therefore, banks will be able to profitably hold 30-year fixed-rate mortgages in portfolio because the interest-rate spread on such loans (the mortgage interest rate minus the covered-bond interest rate) will be established at the time the mortgage is made.

Further, the average life or duration of a 30-year fixed-rate mortgage is much less than 30 years due to periodic principal repayments and mortgage prepayments arising from house sales and mortgage refinances. For example, at a 5% interest rate, the remaining principal balance on a 30-year fixed-rate mortgage will decline by eight percent during the first five years of its life, decline another eleven percent during its second five years, and decline yet another thirteen percent during its third five years. At the end of fifteen years, the principal balance will have been paid down by almost a third; by that time the remaining balance on most 30-year mortgages will have been paid off due to the sale of the home or a mortgage refinance. Hence, 30-year fixed-rate mortgages can safely be financed (i.e., with relatively little maturity mismatching) with covered bonds with maturities of less than 30 years. Maturity mismatches due to the unpredictability of mortgage prepayments can be hedged through interest-rate swaps and other hedging instruments.

Covered-bond financing of home mortgages offers another rarely recognized benefit — the notion of the "conforming" mortgage becomes completely irrelevant. That is the case because there is absolutely no rationale for limiting the size of individual fixed-rate mortgages kept on a lender's balance sheet and funded by covered bonds. This aspect, or really a benefit of covered bonds, makes covered-bond funding of the balance sheets of mortgage lenders especially attractive for areas with high home prices, and therefore large mortgages, such as New Jersey, New York, Massachusetts, and California as well as many large metropolitan areas. In this regard, covered bonds will address one of the major concerns which has been raised about phasing out Fannie and Freddie — funding high-cost mortgages larger than the conforming loan limit.

Covered Bonds Are Not GSE Reform, but Another Horse in the HousingFinance Horse Race

While covered bonds will become an important element of American housing finance, once a strong covered-bond statute is enacted, covered bonds do not represent GSE reform, for the issuance of covered bonds will have no direct bearing on the eventual resolution of Fannie and Freddie. Instead, covered bonds should be viewed as another horse in the housing-finance horse race and a way to bring sound, low-cost financing to American residential finance as well as to other classes of financial assets suitable for covered-bond financing.

Covered Bonds Will Be an Ideal Way to Fund MultiFamily Rental Housing

Covered bonds will provide an excellent source of funding for lender financing of multifamily rental housing for the same reason covered bonds will provide highly efficient funding for owner-occupied homes — covered bonds provide long-term, fixed-rate funding. Sec. 2(8)(C) of H.R. 940 specifies that commercial mortgages shall be an "eligible asset class" for inclusion in a covered-bond cover pool. Sec.2(7)(C) further provides that the commercial mortgage asset class includes "any multifamily mortgage loan." Because borrowers under commercial mortgages usually must pay a prepayment penalty should they refinance the mortgage, prepayments of commercial mortgages are more predictable, which reduces possible maturity mismatches between commercial mortgages of all types and the covered bonds funding those mortgages.

Community Banks Will Be Able to Issue Covered Bonds through the Bill's Pooling Provision

Sec. 2(9) of H.R. 940, which defines the term "eligible issuer," provides in paragraph (D) that an eligible issuer can be a covered-bond issuer "that is sponsored by 1 or more eligible issuers [such as community banks] for the sole purpose of issuing covered bonds on a pooled basis." [emphasis supplied] This provision will enable community banks, and even larger banks, each too small to efficiently sell their covered bonds directly to investors, to join together to sell the covered bonds they have issued into a covered-bond pool that in turn will sell covered bonds to investors. In effect, the covered bonds issued by the pool will be secured by the covered bonds sold into the pool by its participants. The covered bonds sold by a participating bank into the pool would be secured by the assets in that bank's cover pool. Conceivably the creditworthiness of the covered bonds issued by a covered-bond pool could be further enhanced with a third-party credit guarantee.

Covered Bonds Are a "Rates" Product — A Very Desirable Characteristic

Because of their very high creditworthiness — usually AAA — covered bonds are known as a "rates" product. That is, when making investment decisions, investors buying "rates" products are much more concerned about the investment's yield than about the investment's creditworthiness —high credit quality is a must. Because of their structure and statutory protections, covered bonds appeal to those investors who invest only in very high credit-quality securities. Consequently, the interest-rate spread between covered bonds is very close, or "tight," to the yield on government debt. It is reasonable to expect that once a sufficiently large covered-bond market has developed in the United States, which should occur once H.R. 940 is enacted, covered bonds should consistently offer yields roughly comparable to yields on GSE debt. Hence, covered bonds will enable lenders to offer long-term, fixed-rate mortgages at rates comparable to the rates available today on home mortgages eligible for purchase by Fannie and Freddie.

Covered Bonds Can Be Issued by NonBank Financial Firms

Sec. 2(9) of H.R. 940, which defines who can be an "eligible issuer" of covered bonds, provides in paragraph (C) that "any nonbank financial company," as defined in the Dodd-Frank Act, can be a covered-bond issuer. A nonbank financial company in turn is a company with annual gross revenues and consolidated assets equal, respectively, to at least 85% of the company's total gross revenues and assets. Essentially, financial intermediaries who are not banks or bank holding companies can be covered-bond issuers. Nonbank financial companies include insurance companies, the finance subsidiaries of industrial companies, as well as free-standing financial firms, provided they meet the two 85% tests. Authorizing non-bank firms to issue covered bonds will broaden the range of covered-bond issuers, which in turn will provide greater depth and liquidity to the covered-bond secondary market, bringing the efficiencies of covered-bond financing to a broader range of borrowers.

BENEFITS COVERED BONDS WILL DELIVER TO THE U.S. ECONOMY

Widespread use of covered-bond financing will deliver numerous benefits to the U.S. economy, specifically in the safety and efficiency of financing home mortgages and other types of credit that financial intermediaries provide to individuals, families, businesses, and governments. The following is a discussion of the principal benefits.

Better Credit-Risk Management due to Lenders Retaining 100% of the Credit Risk

Better lending will be one of the principal benefits of covered bonds because covered bonds will be backed by loans that lenders make and then keep on their balance sheet rather than selling those loans into the securitization marketplace. Lenders keeping the loans they make will eliminate the moral hazard inherent in the securitization process in which lenders shift the credit risk of the loans being securitized to investors in the liabilities issued by securitization trusts. However, when a lender keeps the mortgages and other loans its makes by funding them with covered bonds, it retains 100% of the credit risk, and 100% of its lending mistakes. That is far preferable to the 5% risk retention mandated for home mortgages by the Dodd-Frank Act.

One supposed benefit of securitization is diversification of credit risk that can arise if a lender is highly concentrated in its geographic credit exposures or borrower types. This can especially be the case with smaller lenders. The problem of insufficient credit-risk diversification by a covered-bond issuer can be dealt with in one or a combination of ways.

First, the lender can enter into credit-default swaps (CDS) to shift an excess of credit-risk concentration to other parties. While CDS have been abused in recent years, notably by AIG, CDS can be a very useful technique for diversifying credit risk away from a lender. CDS would be much less likely to be abused in a covered-bond context than occurred in a securitization context because the party buying the CDS protection actually made the loan and still owns it. This type of CDS transaction also will be much more transparent to investors and to the credit-rating agencies.

Second, investors can demand higher overcollateralization for their covered bonds if they view the lender as having an excess concentration of credit risk. The higher overcollateralization would force the lender to operate with a higher equity-capital ratio so that it would have sufficient equity capital backing its assets not funded by covered bonds.

Third, statutorily authorizing numerous covered-bond asset classes would permit greater asset diversification by lenders. That is, instead of a lender being highly concentrated in just one or two classes of assets funded by covered bonds, the lender could have multiple classes of such assets. That diversity would reduce the need for the lender to purchase CDS protection or to overcollateralize its covered bonds as much as it might have to were it a more narrowly focused lender. This greater diversification will in turn lead to sounder banks and a stronger banking system.

Enhanced Bank Safety-and-Soundness

Covered bonds will enhance bank safety-and-soundness by providing the means for banks to safely fund high-quality assets, such as conservatively underwritten home mortgages. For example, instead of selling the fixed-rated mortgages it originates, thereby weakening its relationship with those borrowers, a bank will be able to keep those mortgages, which will deepen its relationship with its borrower-customers. That stronger relationship will enhance the bank's franchise value.

50 Testimony of Bert Ely

Additionally, the bank will be able to grow its balance sheet, and its revenues, with high-quality mortgages that will strengthen its overall financial condition and profitability. One of the many unfortunate consequences of securitization has been that banks have sold their higher-quality assets while retaining or increasing their focus on riskier lending, such as for land development and construction loans. Covered bonds will permit banks to bring safer, less risky assets back onto their balance sheets, which will greatly enhance the safety and soundness of the U.S. banking system.

Stronger Borrower Protection

As the experience of recent years has taught, asset securitization has led to widespread lending abuses, with borrowers paying the price. The housing bubble which triggered the recent financial crisis and the subsequent foreclosure paperwork crisis, are costly byproducts of those lending abuses.

If a lender can sell a loan soon after it is originated, the lender is much less likely to be concerned about the loan's quality or its impact on the borrower — the lender does not have to eat its cooking. By retaining ownership of a loan, and being fully responsible for any credit losses (to the extent not shifted elsewhere through CDS), lenders will not only be much more careful about the loans they make, but they can be more easily held accountable for their lending abuses because they will still be around, as the owner of the abusive loans. One characteristic of the current crisis is that many lenders who made abusive loans later went out of business because they lacked the capital to repurchase the loans they had sold into the securitization sausage mill.

If Needed, Loan Modifications Are Much Less Complicated

If a lender retains 100% of the credit risk of the loans it makes — the case with loans funded with covered bonds — the lender can more easily modify a loan should the borrower experience financial difficulty. As recent experience has taught repeatedly, loan modification becomes extremely complicated when the lender no longer owns the loan yet the lender or a loan servicer must contend with the legal complexities of modifying a loan owned by a securitization trust which has scores or hundreds of investors, usually in different tranches, and often where some of the interests in that trust having been resecuritized one or several times. In the case of covered-bond financing, by the time a loan reaches the point where it needs to be modified, it has long ceased to be eligible for inclusion in the bonds' cover pool, so the fate of that loan is not of any concern to the owners of covered bonds issued by that lender. The modification impacts only the lender's bottom line.

Foreclosure also would be much simpler because there would be no ambiguity as to who owns the mortgage and who will bear any loss associated with the foreclosure — it will be the lender who bears 100% of the loss. With securitized mortgages, legal questions have arisen as to who owns a mortgage and therefore is entitled to foreclose. That would not be an issue where the lender never sells the mortgage. If the lender purchased CDS protection, the lender might then have to seek some loss recovery from its CDS counterparty, but that would be an event independent of the foreclosure.

Highly Efficient Funding Because of High Credit Ratings, Low Transaction Costs

Covered-bond financing will be highly efficient for two key reasons. First, properly structured covered bonds usually are rated AAA and therefore carry correspondingly low yields relative to lower-rated debt of a comparable maturity. Growth in covered bonds outstanding will increase liquidity in the secondary market for covered bonds, further lowering covered-bond yields.

Second, covered-bond structures are simple and straight-forward relative to asset securitization. Consequently, covered bond issuance is much cheaper that constructing and selling a complicated, multi-tranche asset securitization. Also, paying interest and principal to covered bond investors is much more straight-forward than the management of cash flows during the life of an asset securitization.

Efficient funding will translate into lower borrowing costs. That is, the spread between the interest rate paid by borrowers and the interest rate paid to covered-bond investors will be low or "tight" because the transaction and overhead costs of intermediating funds between the source of funds (covered bonds) and the user of those funds (the borrower) will be lower. Key to that efficient funding, though, is providing legal certainty to covered-bond investors, for that legal certainty will be crucial to covered bonds earning, and keeping, AAA credit ratings.

Reduced Maturity Mismatching by Lenders and an Attendant Reduction in Interest-Rate Risk

Covered bonds generally have "bullet" maturities; i.e., they mature on a pre-established date, with the longest-dated covered bonds having maturities of 15 years, 20 years, or more. Consequently, the maturities of covered bonds can be set to match the scheduled principal amortization and projected prepayments of the mortgages or other types of loans financed by the covered bonds. To the extent needed, the maturity gap between bond maturities and the projected life of the loans can be hedged through the use of derivatives and call options embedded in the bonds.

The wide range of maturities for covered bonds will permit banks and other leveraged lenders to better match the maturities of their assets and liabilities, thereby minimizing maturity mismatching and its associated interest-rate risk, a risk which led to the liquidity crises that have plagued the U.S. financial system in recent years and the S&L crisis of the early 1980s. Covered bonds will be especially well-suited in helping banks to meet the new Basel III liquidity requirements.

A Substantial New Supply of High-Quality Debt for Investors to Purchase

AAA-rated covered bonds will provide investors with a new class of high-quality debt of medium and long-term duration to purchase. Investors will be seeking new classes of high-quality debt as debt issuance by the government-sponsored enterprises[3] (GSEs) contracts, guaranteed liabilities under the FDIC's Temporary Liquidity Guarantee Program mature, and as asset securitization contends with tougher asset-securitization standards. To put this point another way, as covered-bonds grow as a highly rated class of debt, funds will flow to covered bonds as the supply of other types of heretofore highly rated debt shrinks.

This shift towards covered-bond financing will lead to the growth of assets held on bank balance sheets and a corresponding reduction in the size of "shadow banking," which consists principally of asset securitization. As Figure 2 shows, shadow banking has grown in recent decades largely at the expense of banks and other depository institutions. That is, the securitization process shifted loans from bank balance sheets to the balance sheets of

The International Investor Appeal of U.S. Covered Bonds

Because there is a well-developed covered-bond market in Europe, European investors will be prepared to invest in dollar-denominated covered bonds issued by U.S. banks and other institutions — it is an investment class they understand. However, these investors will seek the same assurances and legal protections — safety of principal and timeliness of interest payments in accord with contractual terms — which they have come to expect from the covered bonds in which they now invest. Presumably investors elsewhere, and especially Asian investors, will come to view U.S.issued covered bonds as a safe alternative to U.S. Treasuries and GSE debt.

It is especially important that U.S.-issued covered bonds gain international investor acceptance and appeal as international investors supply a steadily increasing amount of the credit demand in the U.S. economy. As Figure 2 illustrates, the Rest of the World, i.e., non-U.S. investors, now supply almost one-sixth of the total credit outstanding to U.S. borrowers — public and private. According to Federal Reserve Flow of Funds data, foreign investors provided $8.32 trillion, or 15.9% of the credit outstanding in the U.S. economy on September 30, 2010.[4] Given the trade deficits the United States continues to run, that dollar amount and percentage will continue rising for the foreseeable future. Therefore, U.S. borrowers need to increase the supply of highly-rate debt paper they sell to the rest of the world. Covered bonds represent an excellent, efficient way to do so.

SPECIFIC COMMENTS WITH REGARD TO H.R. 940

H.R. 940 is a very good bill. However, I offer the following recommendations to make it an even better bill, thereby creating the statutory framework for a vibrant, efficient U.S. covered-bond market. I have keyed these recommendations to the section and paragraph numbering of H..R. 940, as introduced on March 8, 2011.

Sec. 2(6) — Covered Bond Regulator

I recommend that there be just one regulator for covered bonds and that that regulator be located in the Treasury Department as a subordinate of the Secretary of the Treasury, for the following reasons. Presently, the bill gives the Secretary of the Treasury the authority to establish rules implementing the covered-bond statute, after consulting with the appropriate financial institution regulators, but then delegates the administration of the covered-bond rules to those regulators. Multiple administrators of a common rule will lead to differing interpretations of the rules and potentially to regulatory arbitrage. A single regulator will ensure a much more consistent application of the rules governing covered-bond issuance and administration. However, it would be quite appropriate for the Treasury Secretary to consult with the appropriate safety-and-soundness regulators when formulating the covered-bond rules.

Multiple regulators could be especially detrimental to the pooling of covered bonds by community banks. Because community banks can have one of three regulators — the Fed, the OCC, or the FDIC — it would be difficult for community banks with different primary regulators to join together in one pooling arrangement to issue covered bonds in the name of the pool. That difficulty would lead to an unnecessary fragmentation of the covered-bond market and would be especially harmful to community banks in competing against larger banks which will not have to pool their covered-bond issuances.

Finally, once the covered-bond statute and its rules have been implemented, the regulator is not likely to need a large staff since much of the work of monitoring covered-bonds will be conducted by trustees operating under the terms of covered-bond indentures. Concentrating all regulation of covered bonds in one agency will result in a high-quality staff focused on just one mission — ensuring the smooth and safe operation of the U.S. covered-bond market.

The bank safety-and-soundness regulators would not be left out in the cold. Besides providing input into covered-bond rulemaking, they still could, as safety-and-soundness regulators, supervise the covered-bond issuance of the institutions they regulate, just as they can act to curb any type of risky practice they detect. For example, those regulators could act to enjoin any material maturity mismatching by covered-bond issuers, in accord with the forthcoming Basel III liquidity requirements.

Sec. 2(7) — Eligible Asset

This section of H.R. 940 authorizes numerous types of assets eligible to be financed by covered bonds. Sec. 2(8) then defines the term "eligible asset class," with one class for each type of eligible asset. The argument has been made that some of the types of assets that H.R. 940 makes eligible for covered-bond financing are inappropriate for covered-bond financing, at least initially. Those asset types thought to be inappropriate for covered bond financing include home-equity loans, auto loans, student loans, credit or charge-card receivables, and SBA loans.

A U.S. covered-bond market could launch quite successfully if at least initially eligible assets included only first mortgages on homes, commercial mortgages (including multifamily mortgages), and public-sector loans. It is important to keep in mind that Sec. 2(7)(I) empowers the Secretary of the Treasury to designate other types of assets as eligible for covered-bond financing, which opens the door, once a U.S. covered-bond market has been established, to expand covered-bond financing to home-equity loans, auto loans, student loans, credit or charge-card receivables, and SBA loans.

Sec. 3(B)(3) — Monthly Reporting

In today's Internet world, it makes no sense to require each covered bond issuer to send a monthly report to each owner of the issuer's covered-bonds as to whether the bonds, over the previous month, at all times met the applicable overcollateralization requirements, for two reasons. First, the issuer should merely have to post the required information on a password-protected website that any investor can access at any time. Second, and much more important, the applicable indenture trustee will have a fiduciary obligation to the owners of covered bonds issued under the indenture to monitor the issuer's compliance with all the terms of the indenture agreement, including ensuring that the minimum overcollateralization requirement was met at all times. Therefore, subparagraph (D) in that paragraph can be dropped.

Sec. 3(B)(4)(A) — Independent Asset Monitor Appointment

This subparagraph provides that an issuer of covered bonds shall appoint the indenture trustee for the covered bonds "or another unaffiliated entity" as an independent asset monitor for the applicable cover pool. In my opinion, the indenture trustee should make that appointment since the asset monitor essentially serves as an agent for the trustee in ensuring that the interests of the bond investors are being protected vis-a-vis the covered-bond issuer. Accordingly, the indenture trustee should have the right to replace the asset monitor, or perform that task itself, if it sees fit, without having to obtain the consent of the bond issuer.

Sec. 4(D)(1)(A) — Trustee, Servicer, and Administrator — in General

This subparagraph provide that the covered-bond regulator shall appoint itself or another party as the trustee of any separate covered-bond estate created should a covered-bond issuer be placed in a conservatorship, receivership, liquidation, or bankruptcy proceeding. The grant of this appointment power to the covered-bond regulator is neither necessary nor desirable, for the following reasons.

It is not necessary because there is absolutely no reason why the indenture trustee should not continue, once an estate has been created, as the agent for the bond investors in looking out for their interests. Likewise, the trustee should be the party to appoint a servicer or administrator for the cover pool held by the estate and the party to give notice to the covered-bond regulator that an estate has been created.

The covered-bond investors will be better served by keeping the indenture trustee in place since the trustee is obligated to act in a fiduciary capacity and therefore will have a liability to the bond investors for failing to act properly that the regulator will not have by virtue of the statute's grant of sovereign immunity in Sec. 4(d)(1)(L). At the same time the trustee will be obligated to not act in a manner which unnecessary harms the beneficiaries of the estate's residual interest(s).

Should any creditor of the estate feel the trustee is not performing its duties satisfactorily, that creditor can ask the appropriate court to direct the trustee to act appropriately or the court can replace the trustee.

It is not desirable for the covered-bond regulator to assume any special role with regard to a covered-bond estate as such involvement reinforces the mistaken belief that covered bonds somehow have government support or taxpayer backing. Deleting the authority for the covered-bond regulator to "act as or appoint the trustee for the estate" would go a long way towards undermining that mistaken belief.

Sec. 4(D)(1)(F) — Supervision of Trustee, Servicer, and Administrator

For the reasons just cited, the covered-bond regulator should not be obligated to "supervise the trustee and any servicer or administrator for the estate," as this subparagraph provides.

Sec. 4(D)(2)(D) — Study on Borrowings and Credit

Key to a successful, efficient covered-bond market, and to obtaining high credit ratings for covered bonds, is maintaining the timely flow of principal and interest payments to covered-bond investors, even during stressful economic times. That is, it is not enough that covered-bond investors eventually receive all the principal and interest due them, but that they receive those monies on the day they are due, with no ands, ifs, or buts.

Almost all the time, the cash flows generated by the associated cover-pool assets should be sufficient to pay interest and principal on the covered bonds on time. Further, the issuer can tap other resources to maintain timely payment should the cash flows from the cover-pool assets be insufficient. However, upon the creation of a covered-bond estate, the issuer's resources cannot be tapped to meet principal and interest payment obligations should the cash flow generated by the cover-pool assets be insufficient. The draft legislation wisely authorizes the estate, in Sec. 4(d)(2), to borrow funds "from any person .. solely for the purpose of providing liquidity in the case of timing mismatches among the assets and liabilities of the estate." When financial markets are stable, the estate should be able to borrow sufficient funds from private-sector sources at reasonable rates of interest. However, the need to borrow is unlikely to arise when financial markets are stable and the economy is performing reasonably well. The crunch comes during times of financial instability.

As the recent financial crisis demonstrated, during times of economic stress and distress, asset values decline, cash flows shrivel, and markets freeze. These are the times when central banks must act as lenders of last resort, but without imposing losses on taxpayers. Therefore, the Federal Reserve should be empowered to lend to covered-bond estates, on a conservative senior secured basis, during times of economic stress and distress. Because covered bonds cannot be put back for early prepayment, covered-bond estates will not face massive redemption requests nor will regulators have permitted material maturity mismatching by covered-bond investors, at least between the covered bonds and cover-pool assets. Consequently, liquidity shortfalls in meeting a covered-bond estate's cash-flow obligations should be minor relative to the amount of assets in the applicable cover pool. Therefore, the estate will have ample assets to pledge to the Federal Reserve to collateralize any borrowings, should the need to borrow ever rise.

Although it is highly unlikely that the Fed would ever suffer a loss in lending to a covered-bond estate, the taxpayer can be further protected by authorizing the covered-bond regulator to levy an assessment on all covered-bond issuers, in proportion to the amount of covered-bonds they have outstanding, sufficient to cover the Federal Reserve's loss. Such a lending and assessment authority should replace the study called for by this subparagraph. This assessment authority parallels an assessment authority granted to the FDIC, as will be discussed in the next paragraph. The European experience with covered bonds during the recent financial crisis suggests that it is highly unlikely that the Fed would ever suffer any loss. Instead, it would likely make a substantial profit for taxpayers by providing market support to the covered-bond marketplace during times of great stress and distress.

Sec. 4(D)(6) — No Loss to Taxpayers

As presently drafted, this paragraph would empower the FDIC to recover any losses it might suffer from the failure of a bank which had issued covered bonds. While legitimate in principal, this provision needs substantial modification in two regards. First, the statutory language needs to be more precise as to how the additional loss is calculated that the FDIC suffered by virtue of the failed bank having been a covered-bond issuer. That is, how much higher was the insolvency loss to the bank's unsecured creditors, including the FDIC, due to the presence of covered bonds and the related cover-pool assets on the failed bank's balance sheet?

Second, any such *ex post* assessment must first be offset by the *ex ante* assessments the FDIC will begin collecting on April 1 on bank assets funded by secured borrowings of any type, including covered bonds. That is, in just twenty days, the FDIC will begin collecting deposit-insurance premiums on what effectively are non-deposit bank liabilities. The forthcoming shift in the

FDIC's assessment base, from total domestic deposits, to total assets minus tangible common equity capital, will generate substantial revenues for the FDIC that most likely will far exceed any losses caused by the presence of secured liabilities on bank balance sheets.

Mr. Chairman, I thank you for this opportunity to testify to the Subcommittee today. I welcome the opportunity to answer questions posed by members of the Subcommittee.

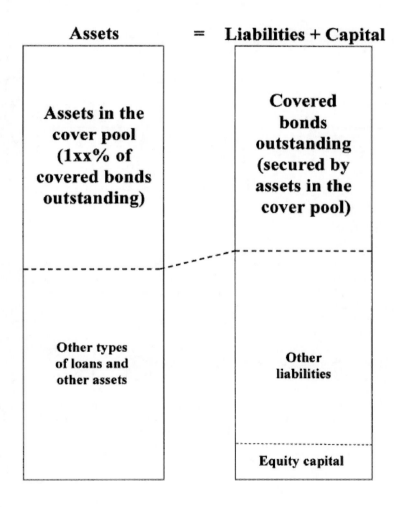

Figure 1. Balance Sheet of a Covered-Bond Issuer.

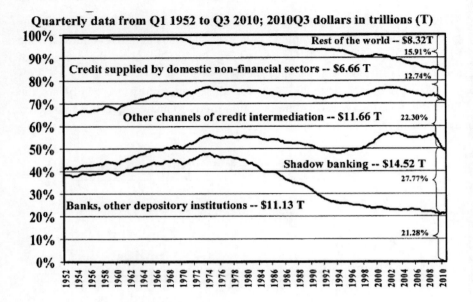

Figure 2. Changes in Credit-Intermediation Shares.

End Notes

[1] Flow of Funds Accounts of the United States, Flows and Outstandings Third Quarter 2010; Federal Reserve statistical release Z.1 (http://www.federalreserve.govireleases/z I /Current/7.1 .pdf); Board of Governors of the Federal Reserve System; December 9, 2010, Tables L. 100, L.101, L.217, and L.218.

[2] Estimated by multiplying total state and local government debt at September 30, 2010, per the Federal Reserve Flow of Funds table L.105 ($2.388 trillion), times local government debt as a percentage of state and local government debt for 2007-08 (60.6%), as reported in the 2008 Census of Government Finance published by the U.S. Census Bureau.

[3] There are five GES: Fannie Mae, Freddie Mac, the Federal Home Loan Banks, the Farm Credit System, and Farmer Mac.

[4] Flow of Funds Accounts of the United States, Flows and Outstandings Third Quarter 2010; Federal Reserve statistical release Z.1 (http://www.federalreserve.gov/releases/z I /Current/z1.pdf); Board of Governors of the Federal Reserve System; December 9, 2010, Table L.1, line 32.

In: Covered Bonds: Features and Proposals ISBN: 978-1-61470-118-7
Editors: Wei Zhao and Chan Li © 2011 Nova Science Publishers, Inc.

Chapter 4

STATEMENT OF TIM SKEET, BOARD MEMBER OF THE INTERNATIONAL CAPITAL MARKET ASSOCIATION[1], BEFORE THE U.S. HOUSE SUBCOMMITTEE ON CAPITAL MARKETS AND GOVERNMENT SPONSORED ENTERPRISES, HEARING ON "LEGISLATIVE PROPOSALS TO CREATE A COVERED BOND MARKET IN THE UNITED STATES"[*]

Mr Chairman and members of the Committee, I am honoured to have the opportunity to discuss with you the European covered bond landscape and how the product fared during and after the crisis.

This testimony provides an overview of the European covered bond market, and is the result of discussions with various European stakeholders, in particular the International Capital Market Association ('ICMA') and one of the Association's subcommittees, which was created nearly two years ago as the Covered Bond Investor Council ('CBIC'). This Council serves to consider issues related to the evolution of the product in Europe and the type of

---

[*] This is an edited, reformatted and augmented version of testimony given by Tim Skeet, Board Member of the International Capital Market Association, before the U.S. House Subcommittee on Capital Markets and Government Sponsored Enterprises, Hearing on "Legislative Proposals to Create a Covered Bond Market in the United States" on March 11, 2011

information available to investors. We have also liaised closely in the preparation of this paper with the European Covered Bond Council ('ECBC')[2], which represents a wide group of market participants.

Our experience in the European Union is that covered bonds did not contribute to fuelling the mortgage or other bubbles and indeed have been consistently regarded as part of the solution to resolving market imbalances, not a cause. This can be explained by the fact that because collateral stays on banks' balance sheets and covered bonds set high collateral quality criteria, the moral and market hazard of the sub-prime mortgage problem was sidestepped. Whereas during the crisis European bank funding relied upon government-insured deposits across the European Union, covered bonds are now perceived as a very stable source of wholesale term liquidity for banks, including for smaller regional institutions, and not exclusively major institutions or too big to fail, 'Strategically Important Financial Institutions' ('SIFIs')[3].

In Europe, it is generally accepted that the covered bond market plays a pivotal role in the exit strategies from government and central bank support. They have provided lenders with a cost-efficient instrument to raise long-term funding and importantly offer private investors non state-guaranteed, top-quality credit exposure to credit institutions. From the consumers' perspective, the success of the covered bond market has ensured a flow of funds to the mortgage sector and helped keep costs down.

PURPOSE OF EUROPEAN COVERED BONDS

Covered bonds have become increasingly important for bank funding in Europe, because they provide low execution risk, long maturities, and help issuers and investors diversify their portfolios of liabilities and assets respectively. Currently investors remain reluctant to buy senior unsecured debt in some jurisdictions, and regulatory discussion of such debt being 'bail-inable' further increases concerns. The structure and security of covered bonds have set this asset class apart and they have remained largely acceptable to investors.

From the issuer's perspective covered bonds offer cheap funding in absolute and relative terms and secondly also offer longer term funding. The success of this funding tool is related to the fact that it has always been difficult to measure the creditworthiness of a bank, and the crisis has only served to reinforce this point in the eyes of many investors. Disillusion with regulators and the credit rating agencies have contributed to an atmosphere of distrust. However, covered bonds represent a form of insurance against the failure of a bank as the bond rating and credit quality is partially delinked from the issuing entity [1][4] by dint of the high quality collateral provided.

As the market for sovereign and agency debt has hit turbulence, new investors came to view covered bonds as offering an acceptable and stable investment opportunity for the cash reserves that had accumulated during the period of market crisis. Moreover, the jumbo market[5] has offered some reasonable liquidity and volume to investors.

The financial crisis has, moreover, highlighted the final major advantage: market accessibility. Although covered bonds clearly did suffer, along with every other asset class, especially in Q4 2008 and in early 2009, there has been a tremendous comeback in terms of spreads and issuance volume as well as investor confidence [1]. Banks can raise term liquidity without running the risk of a failed issue. An absence of defaults, continued strong ratings, lack of the need for official guarantees and strong profit opportunities have driven growth in the market. The ECB purchase programme (see below) helped kick start the restoration of market liquidity for weaker jurisdictions but success has been achieved through the intrinsic qualities of the instrument.

OFFICIAL SUPPORT DURING THE CRISIS

Some observers of the European covered bond market have assumed that the market's success was, and continues to be, due to implicit guarantees by European governments. Whilst it was the case that, at the height of the crisis, all markets for Western financial institutions' debt (and more recently certain government debt) were given varying degrees of support, the strength of the covered bond product is derived from its robust legal framework which explicitly defines and protects investors' rights and not government guarantees or support[6]. Recent discussions around the possibility of extending the burden-sharing concept from hybrid subordinated debt to senior unsecured debt while explicitly excluding covered bonds[7] have further enhanced the attractiveness to and appetite of investors for covered bonds. Regulators and politicians view the European covered bond markets favourably and have taken every opportunity to provide investors with comfort on the safety of the product. This support and confidence has fallen well short of guarantees and the product, post-crisis, does not carry guarantees, explicit or implicit. The essential fact remains that, notwithstanding the drama of the crisis, there has not been any default of principal, or deferment of a covered bond coupon, even where there have been cases of banks failing. Moreover, no significant/systemic downgrade of covered bonds was recorded. As a result no taxpayers' money has been employed to cover covered bond losses. The ultra-conservative eligibility criteria of assets in the cover pool provided stability and have served the product well.

ECB Purchase Programme

In July 2009, as part of the European Central Bank's ('ECB') policies to revive markets and underpin European bank liquidity, a Covered Bond Purchase Programme ('CBPP') was established. This had a finite life of one year and a finite amount of €60bn ($84bn) and was aimed at both primary market (new issues) and secondary paper. The CBPP provided important support in terms of giving private investors confidence as the market recovered [2].

But as publicly stated by the ECB and fully described in their report (published in January 2011) on the impact of the purchase programme [2], their programme *'led to a noticeable broadening of the spectrum of euro area credit institutions that turned to the covered bond product as a funding instrument, which helped increase primary market activity in previously underdeveloped or smaller jurisdictions or segments and revived, at least temporarily, segments that had suffered particularly badly from the financial crisis. These developments contributed significantly to improving the overall funding situation in euro area and also non-euro area financial institutions, and arguably also alleviated some of the pressure on euro-area banks to relay on the Eurosystem's liquidity providing operations'* [2, p.24].

The purchase programme as well as other measures to stabilise financial markets – covered bonds or others – should be considered in the context of governmental steps to stabilise financial markets during the crisis. We also note in this context the unprecedented levels of support provided to the market for certain Western European Government debt – which could expose taxpayers to potential losses. In the ECB's report it is stated clearly that there is an expectation that the programme will prove profitable for the public purse, *'there is a high likelihood that the CBPP will generate positive returns to the Eurosystem'* [2, p.6].

Ratings of Covered Bonds

Part of the collapse in bond prices generally across different markets was provoked by a collapse of investors' confidence in rating agencies and concerns over the underlying asset quality and liquidity of financial issuers. The quality of the legal framework for covered bonds as well as the tight eligibility criteria of the assets in the cover pools on the other hand, has assisted this asset class to address most of the investor concerns, setting covered bonds apart.

Rating agencies still nevertheless play a significant role in the credit assessment of covered bonds, even if investors are now doing far more of their own homework. As result of the crisis, rating agencies have changed and tightened their covered bond rating methodologies. Although this has not resulted in many individual issues actually being downgraded, over-collateralisation levels have been adjusted upwards as a result. Each of the agencies continues to apply their own criteria and there remain important differences between the agencies and the level of de-linkage of the covered bond from the parent stand alone rating.

The question of increased over-collateralisation levels is beginning to be looked at as is the issue of structural subordination of other creditors, although thinking on these matters is still at an early stage. Generally, the rating agencies and European regulators appear, at current encumbrance levels, to appear to favour the covered bond market as contributing vitally to a reduction in systemic risk and increasing term funding in ways that are consistent with current thinking on, for instance, the 'Net Stable Funding Ratio'.

As noted above, European investors are, however, doing a lot more of their own credit analysis on covered bonds in-house, looking at country, legal and credit risks and performing their own assessment of the quality of the cover pool. Efforts are being made in Europe to further enhance transparency and quality of covered bonds. Various discussions are taking place between interested parties including the ECB, ECBC, CBIC and others with a view to arriving at higher disclosure levels, thus allowing investors to better assess underlying risks in the cover pools.

LACK OF DEFINITION OF COVERED BONDS

In European jurisdictions, there is specific legislation setting out a framework for the issuance of covered bonds. Some laws are highly prescriptive (such as German's 'Pfandbriefgesetz'), something generally favoured by European investors, while others are closer to what has been proposed in the US in the past (such as the UK Regulated Covered Bond Law of 2008). There is, however, no universally agreed definition of a covered bond. Indeed, several different types of covered bond have been developed in the European market thus far. The closest to a shared definition is the "Essential features of covered bonds" agreed by the ECBC (see Annex B).

Although the statutory regime in each European jurisdiction differs, all of the regimes incorporate certain core principles: first, covered bonds must be secured by high quality assets; second, management of the cover pools must be supervised; and third, covered bond holders are first in priority upon an issuer bankruptcy or insolvency event. Legislation provides certainty regarding the treatment of covered bonds, especially in an insolvency scenario [3]. The segregation of the cover pool is fundamental to the structure of a covered bond program. The assets comprising the cover pool must be available to ensure that covered bond investors receive scheduled interest and principal payments when due, even if the issuing financial institution is insolvent [4]. Once the covered bond investors are paid off, the residual collateral will be passed back to the insolvency estate for the benefit of the other creditors.

THE IMPORTANCE OF SPECIFIC COVERED BOND LEGISLATION

A key feature of covered bonds and one that clearly distinguishes them from securitisations in particular is that investors' rights are defined by law and not a series of commercial contracts. This is a key point for investors, but the presence of a law does not constitute government guarantees or subsidies for the market. European and indeed US investors buying the product do not view covered bonds as being government supported, but they do see them as being legally robust.

We therefore welcome discussion of a legal-based covered bond structure in the US and the certainty that a law would give investors in terms of their rights to the security of the cover pools. As we have already noted, investors post-crisis have responded in a very positive fashion to the explicit robustness of the product in Europe, which arises from product-level legislation and a specific supervisory structure.

We note also the increasing appetite of US investors for European (and Canadian) covered bonds. We would observe that European issuers are likely to increasingly access the US covered bond market as part of their funding strategy. A number of Nordic issues have tapped the market and France's CFF issued three times in 2010 and has already completed a transaction in 2011. The establishment of a US domestic market would have the beneficial effect of enhancing acceptance of the product in the US, expanding the investor base, but also potentially unlocking European demand for US products. US demand has been fuelled by a lack of strongly rated, high quality 'agency style' assets (diminishing supply of GSE issues, disappearance of TLGP and high investor cash balances). Investors acknowledge that all these instruments implicitly carry credit risk, but US investors are well equipped and increasingly motivated to analyse the component elements of risk that underpin covered bonds. Legislative frameworks do nothing to mitigate credit risk but do serve to mitigate legal and structural risks and ensure that only quality assets may constitute cover pools. US investors have taken note.

The US market experimented with structured covered bonds (i.e. covered bonds that were issued without the benefit of specific legislation) in 2006/2007. However, the structures were cumbersome, costly, cannot be easily replicated today, and do not appeal to investors in Europe or the US. European investors in particular, are unlikely to develop a significant appetite for US covered bonds in the absence of a robust legal framework that only a strong covered-bond statute can provide. The crisis has served to further increase investor concerns over structured covered bonds.

THE IMPORTANCE OF THE COVER POOL: ELIGIBLE ASSETS

European covered bonds offer a very limited variety of collateral for the cover pool and very strict quality criteria. The major categories of cover assets are mortgage loans (including in many cases commercial real-estate) and public sector loans. The range of eligible cover assets is defined by a country's covered bond laws. There has been a strong shift from public sector covered bonds to mortgage covered bonds as the dynamics of profitability and riskiness of public sector lending has changed in recent years. Investors are comfortable with these underlying assets as there is sufficient data and information to allow them to assess the value of collateral. European investors in covered bonds are generally highly conservative and do not currently appear to have much appetite for other underlying asset classes (although there is a very small, local and mainly private placement market in Germany and Denmark for shipping backed covered bonds).

As noted previously, Investors are becoming more vociferous over disclosure levels on cover pools. Although they rely upon public supervision and legal protection, there is now a widespread acceptance in Europe that investors will need to perform their own due diligence and monitoring, something that was rare pre-crisis and this is also further recognition of the resolve not to expose taxpayers' money in future crises within the financial services sector.

AN EXPANDING MARKET

Covered bonds were one of the first non state-guaranteed funding instruments to resume issuance activity after the Lehman default.

The success of the instrument and its role in channelling private funds directly to bank on a term basis has encouraged additional jurisdictions and banks to embrace covered bonds. At least 10 countries are now considering the introduction of covered bonds into their financial systems [1]. Today there are about 25 different European jurisdictions that have active covered bond markets [5]. According to the 2010 ECBC Fact Book [1], there is a strong expectation that the covered bond market will continue to grow, especially as national legislators across Europe have shown a willingness to adapt and update regulations and laws [1], further enhancing the product, at a time of uncertainty over other forms of financial institution funding. Over 30 new issuers joined the market in 2009 alone bringing the total number of issuers to more than 300. Significantly, covered bond jumbo issuance had already reached over 70 bn EUR (US$100bn) by early March 2011, in comparison to €175 bn (US$245bn) for all of 2010 *(See below Table 1)*.

Table 1. Total Jumbo Issuance

EUR bn	2003-2006 average	2007	2008	2009	2010	2011 YTD
Issuance	138	174	93	121	175	70

Source: The Euroweek Cover.

If some of the volume in the primary market was sustained by the ECB Purchase Programme (see above), the high level of activity seen since July 2010 has been purely been sustained by investors working on commercial terms. 2011 is expected to witness record levels of covered bond volumes.

Whilst we do not have any statistics relating to covered bond issuers' size, it is clear through the increase in numbers of issuers during the crisis that far more than just the largest banks have established covered bond programmes. A review of the 17 new issuers since 2010 reveals both large and small banks, jumbo and non-jumbo issuers and includes new ('developing') countries. In some countries, for instance, small regional financial institutions have been able to club together, pool their assets, and benefit from market access (Terra in Norway and Aktia in Finland) including the ability to tap the US investor market (Sparebank 1 of Norway). Regulators have been encouraged by the ability of smaller issuers to make use of this market segment.

MARKET PERFORMANCE AND DATA

The covered bond market was able to generate primary market activity throughout most of the crisis. Evidence suggests that even in times of adverse market conditions, issuers have found it possible to issue covered bonds, particularly in shorter-dated maturities (typically with two year tenors) (see Graph 1). Also in terms of two-way flows, liquidity was concentrated at the shorter-end of the curve. As markets have recovered, covered bonds have taken the lead in providing term-funding to banks, with recent statistics showing that a third of the issues so far in 2011 are of maturities over 10-years for instance, and most issuance is in excess of 5 years.

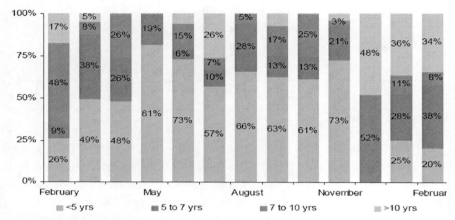

Source: Morgan Stanley.
Note: December 2010 data is not representative as it refers to taps only.

Graph 1. Maturity pattern of newly issued covered bonds, February 2010 to February 2011.

It should be noted also that during the crisis, covered bonds, on account of their acceptability as good collateral with central banks, were used by many financial institutions as a prime source of liquidity through their creation and retention and repoing by issuers [2]. This accounted for a lot of volume issuance (although not counted as 'jumbos'[8]). The market has however rapidly moved on from the repo funding model with increasing numbers of banks able to go directly to private investors with longer term covered bonds, as noted above. The recent success of Spanish banks in this regard is another sign of post-crisis recovery with covered bonds leading the way.

Overall, the secondary market for covered bonds performed better than most other asset classes, although the system of forced market making that used to be at the centre of the 'jumbo' market was suspended early in the crisis and is unlikely to return. The ECB intervention (CBPP, see above) certainly provide a floor for prices and liquidity during the period of its operation, but other markets were similarly sustained by central bank intervention.

The market has emerged post-crisis as the one reliable market for financial institution debt and is enjoying an expansion of its investor base. The market consensus in Europe is that though liquidity has not returned to the pre-crisis levels, the primary market for covered bonds is robust, albeit at wider spread levels compared to before.

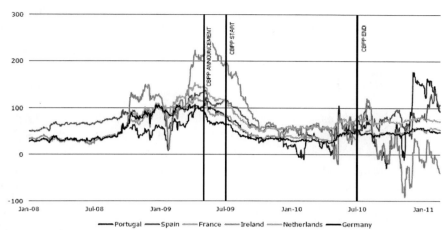

Source: ECB.
Note: All spreads refer to the IBoxx indices for 5-year maturity.

Graph 2. Covered Bond spreads vis-a-vis sovereign yields.

Source: iBoxx, Credit Agricole CIB.

Graph 3. Covered Bond Spreads, 2007-10, in basis points.

Investors remain concerned about sovereign risk and this has recently helped parts of the covered bond market.

According to a Fitch report [6] published in February 2011, when asked to rank the main challenges that they see ahead for the market, 37.2% of the investors surveyed put sovereign risk at the top of the list, while 20.5% had concerns regarding the performance of the assets in cover pools. The health of the banking sector and the liquidity of the secondary market are the main concerns for 15.4% of investors. 7.7% of investors fear regulatory chances related to the implementation of Basel III and Solvency II. However, overall, the majority of investors who responded (82.9%) are planning either to maintain their current covered-bond holdings or to increase them.

Stable Investor Base

Covered bonds have long had a very stable investor base that values the qualities of the product. Even during the crisis, the distribution statistics of jumbo covered bond transactions did not materially change, with all the major classes of investor all continuing to purchase covered bonds throughout the crisis and this in a context of issuance volumes being maintained or increasing. This was one of the factors that helped to ensure that spreads in the covered bond market were much more stable than in other parts of the capital market.

Even at the height of the crisis the overall investor base for covered bonds remained largely intact (although the appetite for certain jurisdictions did matter). Indeed there has been strong demand for small, non-'jumbo' transactions, something which has greatly aided issuer funding flexibility and asset/liability matching. Graph 3 (below) shows the make-up of the investor market from 2007 to date.

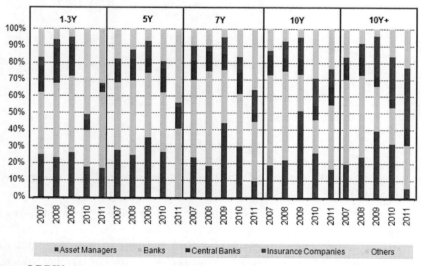

Source: LBBW.

Graph 4. Distribution of Jumbo issues by investor type per maturity bank (%).

Table 2. Total Covered Bond Issuance (including jumbos)

EUR bn	2003-2006 average	2007	2008	2009
Issuance	435	464	651	529

Source: ECBC.

IN CONCLUSION

European covered bonds are not new, nor do they constitute "financial engineering". In various formats, covered bonds have been used in Europe for centuries without bonds holders suffering defaults or credit losses. The success of the European covered bond market during and post-crisis can be attributed to many factors: firstly, the legal frameworks under which covered bonds are created, secondly the quality of the assets in the cover pool and the narrow list of eligible assets; and finally the hard-wiring of the product in the European legislation and the positive regulatory treatment that covered bonds has been received. This has been achieved without taxpayers' money being exposed to loss.

Covered bonds enjoyed support during the crisis in line with support to all areas of the financial markets. The nature of the instrument itself has given significant comfort to investors. The very rapid recovery of the covered bond market post-crisis is confirmation that this asset class did not expose taxpayers to losses and continues to play an important part in the mobilising of private sector funding for mortgages and public sector lending. With the end of the ECB CBPP, covered bonds remain a growing market in which investors have confidence and where governments do not need to provide support. Covered bonds in Europe have been a solid part of the solution to the crisis, not a contributor to, or part of the cause.

ANNEX A. THE INTERNATIONAL CAPITAL MARKET ASSOCIATION

The International Capital Market Association (ICMA) is the trade association representing constituents and practitioners in the international capital market worldwide. ICMA performs a crucial central role in the market by providing a framework of industry-driven rules and recommendations which regulate issuance, trading and settlement in international fixed income and related instruments. ICMA liaises closely with regulatory and governmental authorities, both at the national and supranational level, to ensure that financial regulation promotes the efficiency and cost effectiveness of the capital market.

ANNEX B. ECBC ESSENTIAL FEATURES OF COVERED BONDS [8]

The ECBC sets out what it considers to be the essential features of covered bonds, together with explanatory notes. These common essential features should be understood as the ECBC's minimum standards for covered bonds and have to be read independently from any other definition or interpretation of covered bonds, such as those set out in the Undertakings for Collective Investment in Transferable Securities (UCITS) directive and in the Capital Requirements Directive (CRD)[9]. [8]

The essential features which has been isolated and which are achieved under special-law-based framework or general-law-based framework are the following: [8]

1) The bond is issued by – or bondholders otherwise have full recourse to – a credit institution which is subject to public supervision and regulation.
2) Bondholders have a claim against a cover pool of financial assets in priority to the unsecured creditors of the credit institution.
3) The credit institution has the ongoing obligation to maintain sufficient assets in the cover pool to satisfy the claims of covered bondholders at all times.
4) The obligations of the credit institution in respect of the cover pool are supervised by public or other independent bodies.

The ECBC database (www.ecbc.eu) offers a unique way to easily access and compare technical details between different covered bond frameworks. The database can also be seen as a contribution towards transparency as well as helping to picture what constitutes a covered bond.

ANNEX C. COVERED BONDS DEFINITION UNDER CRD AND UCITS

Two sets of European directives – UCITS and CRD – regulate the prudential treatment of covered bonds. Although these two directives are primarily aimed at providing harmonisation for the purposes of prudential regulation of banks and UCITS, these two EU directives are essential to understanding the main features and risk profiles of covered bonds. In addition, national legislation gives the basic framework to national covered bonds, particularly the general requirements for issuer banks, the competences of authorities and other entities responsible for controls, and provisions aimed at ensuring ring-fencing of assets and investors' rights in the event of bankruptcy. At the national level, the secondary legislation enacted by government and/or supervisory bodies, lays down more detailed rules on matters such as eligibility requirements, minimum collateralization levels, asset and liability management, and the checks to be carried out.

First, the special character of covered bonds has been enshrined in the Article 52 (4) of the UCITS Directive 2009/65/EC. Article 52 (4) does not mention the name "Covered Bond", but defines the minimum requirements that provide the basis for privileged treatment of bonds which are secured by assets. The European Central bank also classifies securities for repo purposes. Banks, which comprise a significant portion of the covered bond investor base, tend to hold covered bonds as collateral for their repo activities. For this purposes, the ECB follows the covered bond definition used in the UCITS directive. In order to have an EU recognised "covered bond" regime, a country must implement the requirements of Article 22(4) of the UCITS Directive, which essentially include covered bonds issued under statutes imposing special bankruptcy protection for covered bond holders [3].

Covered bonds that comply with Article 52 (4) UCITS directive are considered as a particular safe investment, which can explain the easing of prudential investment limits. Therefore, investment funds (UCITS) can invest up to 25% (instead of a maximum of. 5%) of their assets in covered bonds of a single issuer that meet the criteria of Article 52 (4). Similar, the EU Directives on Life and Non-Life Insurance (Directives 92/96/EEC and 92/49/EEC) allow insurance companies to invest up to 40% (instead of a maximum of 5%) in UCITS-compliant covered bonds of the same issuer [1].

A second cornerstone of covered bond regulation at EU level is the Capital Requirement Directive (CRD). The CRD is based on a proposal from the Basel Committee on Banking Supervision to revise the supervisory regulations governing the capital adequacy of internationally active banks. The CRD rules apply to all credit institutions and investment service providers in the EU [1]. The special treatment of covered bonds is an important feature of the CRD as it goes beyond the Basel II framework. With regard to covered bonds, CRD refers to the criteria of the UCITS Directive of 1985. Beyond this legal definition, a series of eligibility criteria for cover assets were stipulated. [8]

Asset Encumbrance

In most EU jurisdictions there are no specific limits placed on asset encumbrance or concerns around depositors and/or unsecured subordination. There has been some work done by the FSA in the UK which resulted in guidance on the amount of covered bonds a bank could issue (4% notification level and 20% asset soft cap). Any discussion of this subject should be looked at in the context of the overall Basel III/CRD capital requirements ratio and regulatory triggers currently being drawn up and put in place to prevent the collapse of a financial institution in the future. It was widely recognised in the EU that covered bonds have been part of the solution and not the problem in the market. And that uncertainty of the senior unsecured debt is further underpinning the demand of investors for covered bonds. We recognise that in some jurisdictions, including the United States, thought is being given to regulatory limits on issuance but they should not be drawn up in such a way that they preclude the development of a covered-bond market.

ANNEX D. REGULATORY TREATMENTS OF COVERED BONDS

Ongoing regulatory reform, notably the Basel III agreement, amendments to the Capital Requirement Directive (CRD) and Solvency II, are likely to affect covered bonds [6]. The main component of Basel III's liquidity regime is the Liquidity Coverage Ratio (LCR). The LCR requires banks to maintain a stock of "high-quality liquid assets" that is sufficient to cover net cash outflows for a 30-day period under a stress scenario. In its initial consultative document[10], the Basel Committee defined "high-quality liquid assets" *extremely* conservatively. Banks' liquidity pools have to be at least 60% Level 1 assets (cash, central bank reserves, and sovereigns) and no more than 40% Level 2 assets (GSE obligations, and non-financial corporate or covered bonds rated AA- or above). The Basel III framework presents that a minimum 15% haircut should be applied to the current market value of each Level 2 assets, such as covered bonds – without any consideration of the underlying maturity. According to the Net Stable Funding ratio (NSFR), as specified in the Basel III framework, covered bonds as assets held in the cover pool are encumbered are given a Required Stable Funding (RSF) factor of 100%. A 65% RSF factor is applied to unencumbered mortgages.

EU banks must also comply with the new proposals contained in CRD 2 and CRD 3 in order to benefit from lower capital charges[11]. Future liquidity ratio regulation may also shift some demand towards covered bond markets, as the latter receive a more favourable treatment for liquidity purpose than the former [9].

Insurance companies and pension funds, in so far they invest on general account and not on behalf of third parties, will also have to comply with Solvency II capital charges. Market commentators argue that the higher capital charges on ABSs in Solvency II may make it less attractive for insurers and pension funds to invest in them than in covered bonds, bank floating rate notes or senior unsecured bonds [9].

REFERENCES

[1]   ECBC Fact Book, 2010 edition

[2]   European Central Bank, *'The impact of the Eurosystem's covered bond purchase programme on the primary and secondary markets'*, Occasional Papers Series, no 122, January 2011

[3]   Pinedo, Anna, T. And Tanenbaum, James, R. Morrison & Foester LLP, *"Lucrative knock-offs: Covered bonds in the US"*, Global Banking and Financial policy review, 2005.

[4]   Clifford Chance, *"US Covered Bonds – Proposed Legislation Introduced to Encourage Market Development"*, Client Memorandum April 2010.

[5]   European Central Bank, *"Covered Bonds in the EU Financial System"*, Eurosystem Publication, December 2008.

[6]   Fitch Ratings, *Covered Bonds Investor Survey, EMEA Special Report,* February 2011

References

[7] European Covered Bond Council, "*ECBC Essential Features of Covered Bonds*", available at http://ecbc.hypo.org/ content/default. asp?PageID=367

[8] European Covered Bond Council, "*Introducing covered bonds*", available at http://ecbc.hypo.org/Content/Default.asp?PageID=504

[9] European Covered Bond Council, "*ECBC Position Paper on CRD IV: arguments and supporting evidence*", available at http://intranet.hypo.org/docs/1/CMCACNACFIHFACAOMFLKJMKNP DWY9DBDBKTE4Q/EMF/Docs/DL S/2011-00004.pdf

[10] European Central Bank, "*Recent Developments in Securitisation*", Eurosystem Publications, February 2011.

End Notes

[1] See Annex A

[2] The European Covered Bond Council represents the covered bond industry, bringing together covered bond issuers, analysts, investment bankers, rating agencies and a wide range of interested stakeholders. The ECBC was created by the European Mortgage Federation (EMF) in 2004 to represent and promote the interests of covered bond market participants at the international level. As of February 2011, the ECBC has over 100 members from more than 25 active covered bonds jurisdictions. ECBC members represent over 95% of the €2.4 trillion covered bonds outstanding.

[3] Systemically Important Financial Institutions

[4] Numbers in brackets refer to documents listed as references at the end of this statement.

[5] for issue over €1bn or US$ 1bn in size

[6] Although in the case of Ireland an explicit guarantee was granted and other governments had been ready to provide guarantees as in the case of Germany, this was not needed so none were provided.

[7] See European Commission (2011), *Consultation on technical details of a possible European crisis management framework*, Internal Market and Services DG, Unit H1 – Banking and Financial conglomerates

[8] Covered bond transactions totaling €1 billion or more

[9] See 2006/49/EC and 2006/49/EC.

[10] BIS (2009), Consultative Document: International Framework for liquidity risk measurement, standards and monitoring, Basel Committee on Banking Supervision, December 2009.

[11] CRD 2: Directive 2009/111/EU and Directive 2009/83/EU amending the CRD. CRD 3: Proposed directive amending CRD (in relation to trading book activities). CRD comprises the Banking Consolidation Directive (Recast) 2006/48/EC and the Capital adequacy Directive (Recast) 2006/48/EC.

In: Covered Bonds: Features and Proposals ISBN: 978-1-61470-118-7
Editors: Wei Zhao and Chan Li © 2011 Nova Science Publishers, Inc.

Chapter 5

STATEMENT OF RALPH DALOISIO, MANAGING DIRECTOR, NATIXIS, ON BEHALF OF THE AMERICAN SECURITIZATION FORUM, ASF COVERED BONDS SUBFORUM, BEFORE THE U.S. HOUSE SUBCOMMITTEE ON CAPITAL MARKETS AND GOVERNMENT SPONSORED ENTERPRISES, HEARING ON "LEGISLATIVE PROPOSALS TO CREATE A COVERED BOND MARKET IN THE UNITED STATES"[*]

Chairman Garrett, Ranking Member Waters, and Distinguished Members of the Subcommittee, I thank you for this opportunity to testify before you today.

---

[*] This is an edited, reformatted and augmented version of testimony given by Ralph Daloisio, Managing Director, Natixis, on behalf of the American Securitization Forum, ASF Covered Bonds Subforum, before the U.S. House Subcommittee on Capital Markets and Government Sponsored Enterprises, Hearing on "Legislative Proposals to Create a Covered Bond Market in the United States" on March 11, 2011.

PREAMBLE

The American Securitization Forum (the "ASF") was formed to enable participants in the US securitization industry to pursue a mission of education, consensus, and advocacy on matters relating to the form and function of the US securitized debt capital markets. The ASF has over 330 institutional members engaged in every significant aspect of this market—issuers, investors, servicers, dealers, ratings agencies, law firms, trustees, and a variety of data and technology vendors. Assuming a legislated US covered bond market is established, our members will have a leading and lasting role in this new financial instrument, much like they did over 25 years ago with the creation of the first asset-backed security.

As the current Chair of the ASF Board of Directors, a former Chair of the ASF Investor Committee, and as a Managing Director of Natixis, I offer testimony today in support of a promising legislative framework for covered bonds in the United States. In particular, I seek to represent the views of institutional investors, who could bring the necessary capital to invest in this product. By way of background, the ASF Investor Committee represents over 60 pension fund, mutual fund and insurance company member institutions, who collectively manage trillions of dollars of Main Street's financial investments. The institution I am employed with, Natixis, is the commercial and investment banking subsidiary of BPCE, the second largest bank in France as measured by retail deposits. Natixis and its affiliates have held a long-standing leadership role in the European covered bond market, acting as an issuer, dealer, and investor and conduct significant investment and banking activities in the United States. My professional experience in securitized debt capital markets and related investment activity covers the past 20 years.

The right kind of legislation, like the legislation you Chairman Garrett and Congresswoman Maloney have introduced on Tuesday, has the power to create a new channel of efficient credit flow through our financial system while facilitating an accelerated and more orderly exit of US government financial support for the private sector. The proposed legislation would create a new and disciplined market structure around which free market forces can organize to better balance the flow of money, capital, and credit in our highly sophisticated financial system. The concentrated US banking system market structure invites the creation of new financing channels, so we can better democratize the flow of credit to Main Street in an effort to improve its post-crisis affordability and accessibility to American consumers and businesses. Credit democratization is something the securitization markets have been particularly effective in doing, but additional forms of financing are necessary to support appropriate levels of credit creation in the US. As such, we fully support your initiative to establish a new credit channel for the ultimate benefit of Main Street.

THE SHORT HISTORY OF US COVERED BONDS

It appears ironic to acknowledge that US covered bonds have already been issued, without legislation. As many of you may know, the first US insured depository institution ("IDI") covered bond was issued by Washington Mutual ("WaMu") nearly 5 years ago, even without a legislative framework for it. Approximately a year later, Bank of America became the second US bank to issue covered bonds. In the absence of any legislative framework in the United States, these issuances were denominated in Euros and sold predominantly into the European covered bond market as "contractual" covered bonds.

In July 2008, the FDIC published a Final Statement of Policy (the "Final Policy") for the exercise of its receivership and conservatorship authority in respect of covered bond contracts entered into by a US IDI and the US Treasury issued its "Best Practices for Residential Covered Bonds Guidelines"[1] (the "Best Practices Guidelines") for the issuance of contractual US covered bonds in coordination with the FDIC's Final Policy. At the time, Treasury believed a framework defined by policy and regulation[2] would be sufficient to initiate a US covered bond market that could restore the financing that was withdrawing from a declining asset securitization market. This belief was disproved quickly as the financial crisis accelerated into the autumn and culminated with historic emergency measures passed by Congress. Just two months after the Treasury and FDIC frameworks were issued, Washington Mutual was closed by the OTS and the FDIC was appointed receiver. During those two months, secondary market prices of WaMu's Euro-denominated covered bonds fell precipitously as holders of those investments began to focus on the risk that the FDIC's repudiation authority could override contractual protections while the value of the residential mortgages in the covered pool would decline. Historical price data indicate that the WaMu covered bonds traded as low as 75 cents on the dollar, before rallying after the acquisition by J.P. Morgan later that same September in 2008.[3] The 2006 and 2007 issuances by WaMu and Bank of America remain the only US covered bond issues to date. Curiously, no US covered bonds were issued after the

FDIC published its Final Policy and the US Treasury published its Best Practices Guidelines.

POLICY AND REGULATION ARE INSUFFICIENT TO SUPPORT A U.S. COVERED BOND MARKET

The experience of investors in WaMu covered bonds highlighted the weakness in relying on a regulatory, rather than a legislative, framework for US covered bonds. In general, regulatory frameworks are more easily revised than legislative frameworks, which would require an act of sovereign government to change, rather than a regulatory action under the regulator's own control. Consequently, regulatory frameworks are more susceptible to whim or political expediency that can be disruptive of markets and injurious to investors who relied on such frameworks. In particularly good times, investors might be willing to overlook or de-emphasize the risk posed by a regulatory regime, buy the bonds, and accept even an insignificant premium for the incremental risk. This is basically what occurred in the WaMu story. When stress arises, however, at the precise moment that a framework needs to show stability and resilience, markets will focus their attention on the weaknesses and extract a sometimes painful toll for their sheer presence. If we are to start a new and promising financial sector, we can ill-afford to marry it to a weak legal framework. The centerpiece of any legal framework will be that framework's treatment of covered bonds in the event of an issuer's insolvency.

THE NEED TO CURB FDIC INSOLVENCY RESOLUTION AUTHORITIES BY PASSING US COVERED BOND LEGISLATION

In a prospective US covered bond market, the FDIC would be the operative regulator for IDIs that choose to issue covered bonds. Our expectation would be for much of the early US covered bonds market to be developed by US banks, given the experience in other countries. As it now stands, the FDIC's authority as receiver or conservator is simply contradictory and counterproductive to the creation of a healthy legal framework for a covered bond market. This is because the FDIC has too much discretion to choose among resolution alternatives that would have varying consequences for covered bondholders, especially including the worst-case outcome that the FDIC could elect to repudiate a covered bond contract, determine the fair market value of the cover pool securing the covered bonds, and pay covered bondholders the lesser of par or cover pool fair market value with interest accrued only through the date of the FDIC's appointment as receiver, and not to the date on which investors are actually repaid.

Even if the FDIC were to promulgate guidance limiting itself to its more investor-friendly bank such self-governed guidance. This is because the FDIC would have an inherent conflict of interest to take action that minimizes losses to the Depositary Insurance Fund ("DIF"), regardless of whether such result came at the expense of secured creditors. Such conflict of interest was amplified in acts of earlier Congresses requiring the FDIC to use the "least costly" transaction(s) for resolving insolvent IDIs and giving depositors a payment priority over other unsecured creditors of an insolvent bank. This being the case, legislation is required to limit the FDIC's optionality in resolving the covered bond contracts of a bank under the receivership or conservatorship control of the FDIC. Allowing the FDIC to retain its current authority under Section 11(e)(12) of the Federal Deposit Insurance Act ("FDI Act") in respect of an IDI's secured indebtedness for covered bonds would be a grave policy misstep in our view, and would undermine the market before it can be developed. In the opinion of our issuer and investor members, covered bond legislation needs to set a clear and unmistakable set of resolution mechanics that assure investors will receive the economic value of a market-based negotiation of contracts consistent with the principles already in long-standing operation around the globe for this type of indebtedness. Only legislation can create a carve out for covered bonds in order to curb the insolvency authorities the FDIC now has over covered bonds to the extent necessary to establish a US legislative framework that is competitive with the more established programs domiciled elsewhere.

CONCERNS THAT COVERED BOND LEGISLATION WOULD INCREASE THE RISK OF LOSS TO THE DEPOSITARY INSURANCE FUND AND TO THE U.S. TAXPAYER ARE MISPLACED

Some fear that an investor-friendly US covered bond legislation would pose greater risks to the FDIC DIF and ultimately to the US taxpayer. We believe any such fears are misplaced, especially since, by the FDIC's own account, Dodd-Frank has "granted the FDIC the ability to achieve goals for [DIF] fund management that it has sought for decades but lacked the tools to accomplish"[4]. Among other things, Dodd-Frank raised the minimum designated reserve ratio ("DRR"), removed its upper limit, eliminated the requirement that the FDIC dividend amounts when the DRR is between 1.35% and 1.5%, granted the FDIC sole authority to determine dividend policy above a DRR of 1.5%, and set the calculation of insurance premiums against total assets, not total deposits.[5] Accordingly, it would seem more logical for the FDIC to adjust deposit insurance premiums to the asset-liability practices of IDIs, including any covered bond issuance practices, rather than seek to maintain their traditional insolvency authorities which could impede or even prevent a US covered bond market from becoming a feature of our credit system. Perhaps even the FDIC has come to recognize this in a post Dodd-Frank world, as the September 15, 2010 testimony of the FDIC before the Senate Banking Committee includes a sentence whereby the FDIC witness Michael Krimminger, currently the FDIC's General Counsel, states, "[t]he FDIC would support covered bond legislation that clarifies the amount of repudiation damages to be the par value of outstanding bonds plus interest accrued through the date of payment."[6] Such a policy stance would be a significant improvement from the FDIC's Final Policy wherein the FDIC takes the position that repudiation would mean a payment equal to the lesser of par or the fair market value of the cover pool, plus bond interest accrued to the date on which the FDIC was appointed receiver. This Final Policy subjects investors to market-value loss on the cover pool and could additionally cause a period of lost interest payments for investors. While such movement in policy stance is encouraging, it does not go far enough as the FDIC would still retain an option that is exercisable against investors: *if the cover pool were unhealthy*, the FDIC would turn the cover pool over to an estate for the benefit of covered bondholders who would likely encounter a loss and a resulting unsecured deficiency claim against the issuer; *if the cover pool were healthy*, the FDIC would liquidate it, capture the excess collateral value for the insolvent estate, and pay par to investors, exposing them to what could be potentially material re-investment risk. Still, the movement in the FDIC's policy stance is encouraging in that it signals further movement could occur in favor of a globally competitive US covered bond framework.

THE GLOBAL NATURE OF A SUBSTANTIAL COVERED BOND MARKET

Like so many financial markets today, the covered bond market is a global market, though it remains concentrated in its European geography of origin. Covered bonds date back to 18th century Prussia, when the Pfandbriefe was introduced by the decree of King Frederick the Great to enable the property of nobles to be pledged as collateral to investors in exchange for agricultural credit. The German Mortgage Bank Act of 1900 modernized the original concept by creating a formal legal framework that assured the cover pool would be ring-fenced on an issuer's balance sheet and that investors in covered bonds had recourse to both the cover pool and the issuer in the event of a default[7]. The first issue of French legal covered bonds (Obligations Foncières) was created by decree in 1852 by Crédit Foncier de France under the *société de credit Foncier* statute. The main business of Crédit Foncier de France, founded in 1852, is to grant mortgage-backed real estate loans and local authority loans and to issue bonds to finance these loans.[8]

Today, some 29 countries are counted as having covered bond frameworks rooted in regulation, contract law, or legislation. 22 countries now have legislated covered bond market structures, with Australia, Canada, and New Zealand in the process of passing legislation for covered bonds[9]. Germany, Spain, Denmark, France, and the UK represent nearly 80% of the outstandings of covered bonds.[10] The Euro is the predominant currency in which covered bonds are issued, and there are between 140 and 150 issuers of Euro-benchmarked covered bonds.[11]

There is a clear preference for legislative (or statutory) covered bond frameworks. Of the estimated €2.5 trillion in outstanding covered bonds, an estimated 92% were issued under legislative frameworks. A central feature of statutory frameworks concerns the legal framework for insolvency of the covered bond issuer. Effective legislative frameworks include a specific legal framework superseding the general insolvency law. The typical legal framework under legislated market structures affords investors dual recourse: recourse to the cover pool as a secured creditor and recourse to the issuer as an unsecured creditor for amounts not repaid by the cover pool. Of additional importance, the insolvency of the issuer does not automatically trigger the acceleration of the covered bond indebtedness and an accompanying liquidation of the cover pool. This last feature mitigates reinvestment risk, or the risk that an issuer's insolvency would trigger a prepayment to covered bond investors that at a given moment could not be reinvested for comparable investment return to that of the prepaid covered bonds.

The economic benefits of a country's covered bond program can be significant. Market research shows that banks issuing covered bonds can save between 20 and 60 basis points per year on interest rates when compared to the rates paid on their senior unsecured issues of comparable maturity[12]. Such savings can be transmitted through society in the form of lower rates on the consumer and commercial credit that finances our economy, stimulates growth, and creates jobs.

During periods of economic stress, the relative differential between secured and unsecured borrowing costs increases. Over the past year, such differential expanded to over 4% per annum for weaker banks operating in stressed economies.[13] The ability to issue relatively lower-cost financing, which becomes increasingly relative lower-cost financing during periods of worsening economic and financial stress, is a distinguishing benefit of covered bonds.

THE BARREN BUT RAPIDLY CHANGING LANDSCAPE FOR US COVERED BONDS AND THE INVESTMENT MARKET'S NEED FOR HIGHLY-RATED FIXED INCOME PRIVATE SECTOR INVESTMENT

Since the US Treasury, in coordination with the FDIC, issued guidelines in support of establishing a US covered bond market, there has been no issuance of a covered bond by a US issuer. Part of this absence may be explained by the limited investor appetite for exposure to U.S. residential mortgage loans not guaranteed by one of the GSEs (residential mortgage loans are, by far, the primary type of collateral in cover pools worldwide). Part of this absence may also be explained by the continuing role of the GSEs and FHA, which have been responsible for 95% of all new residential mortgage loans having been made in the US in these recent years. Part of the absence may also be explained by the repaired balance sheets of US banks, which have shown a limited need for securitization or secured financing in the face of a rising deposit base.

But the landscape is changing rapidly. Although there was only one US$ issuance of a covered bond in 2009—which took place outside the United States-2010 saw a huge increase in US$ issuance of covered bonds. 21

covered bond issues were denominated in US$ in 2010, from issuers based in France, Germany, the United Kingdom, Sweden, Norway and the Netherlands. 2010 US$ covered bond issuance aggregated $30 billion, beginning a trend that has been continuing into 2011[14]. Our neighbors to the North, in Canada, issued 9 of these 21 US$ deals in 2010, aggregating half the total 2010 US$ issuance volume. They issued at rates of interest that were materially lower than other US$ issuers, which is attributable to the extremely low risk of the collateral in their cover pools, which consists of Canadian residential mortgage loans that are guaranteed by Canada Mortgage and Housing Corp., the "AAA" rated full faith and credit Canadian Government agency. In short, our US$-based investors have been investing noticeably in US$ covered bonds for over a year now, but they have been buying them from non-US issuers.

When the approach taken by Treasury to implement a policy framework for contractual covered bond issuance by US issuers failed to gain traction, ASF membership was very supportive of your efforts Chairman Garrett for a legislative response. In March 2010, the United States Covered Bond Act of 2010 was introduced, which was the right idea at the right time, as the market has already validated the movement towards US dollar-denominated covered bonds even before US legislation has passed. We can now interpret this movement as an invitation to pass legislation, which could have a positive transformative effect on the US banking and financial system. Asset securitization was the primary manufacturer of "AAA" rated private-sector investments, but the post-crisis issuance of "AAA" rated securities has dropped to a fraction of its pre-crisis volume. It is clear that non-US issuers are tapping into the US investor demand for high-quality investments like those offered under existing covered bond frameworks. The ASF voices its full support for such an enacting piece of legislation.

ASF RECOMMENDATIONS IN SUPPORT OF EFFECTIVE US COVERED BOND LEGISLATION

In contemplating the United States Covered Bond Act of 2011 and in considering the type of legislation that would be most constructive to the emergence of a deep and liquid US covered bond market, the members of the ASF would like to articulate some principles that we believe should be present in the legislation.

In particular, effective legislation in favor of covered bonds should be as investor-friendly as possible. Many institutional investors in the US and abroad are living with the painful memory of recent government-sponsored intervention that has compromised the operation of contracts. Moreover, the attempt by some regulators to exercise expansive authority over the efficacy of certain debt capital markets products also threatens the confidence investors have in government- led market initiatives. A striking recent example of this expansive view is the securitization safe harbor rules which have been promulgated by the FDIC. The FDIC has publicly stated that such rules are intended to protect the investors in future asset-backed securities sponsored by IDIs, but in fact it will be the investors who lose the protection of an insolvency-remote true sale if the affected IDI failed to meet or comply with the requirements of the securitization safe harbor over which investors have no control.

ASF submits the following essential principles that we believe should be present in the legislation, among others:

1) **The legislation should allow for bank and non-bank entrants without discriminating on the basis of size or credit quality.** Investors should be afforded a menu of alternative covered bonds, which includes multiple issuers of varied standing. This would allow a more balanced flow of capital into the credit sector and avoid imbalances and over-investment in a small number of issuers and too few covered bond programs. It also would avoid the pitfall of having legislation pick the "winners" and "losers."

2) **The legislation should allow a wide variety of collateral types to be included in the cover pool.** Such optionality would allow for investor choice and market-based preferences to balance the flow of capital into an emergent US covered bond sector. Collateral types could include residential mortgage loans, loans outstanding under home equity lines of credit, multi-family housing loans, commercial mortgage loans, auto loans, auto leases, student loans, consumer credit card loans, public sector loans, other types of loans deemed appropriate by the supervising authority, and securities backed by any of the foregoing collateral types provided the security is not backed by more than one, homogenous collateral type.

3) **The legislation should not allow different types of collateral to be co-mingled in the same cover pool, but instead require asset type homogeneity within a cover pool.** This will facilitate elegant

simplicity and create standardization and enhanced transparency from the investment perspective. As the U.S. emerges from a rather opaque, complex, and non-standard system of mortgage securitization, aspects of a new secured finance system would find greater uptake in biasing themselves to enhanced simplicity, standardization, and the resulting improvement in transparency.

4) **The legislation must allow investors full dual recourse: first, to the cover pool as a primary source of payment for principal and interest on the covered bonds, and second, as unsecured creditors to the issuer in the event the cover pool proceeds are insufficient to repay principal and interest in full on the covered bonds.** A covered bond investor's unsecured claim should rank *pani passu* with the other senior, unsecured claims on the issuer. Dual recourse is, in fact, 100% "skin-in-the-game". The bank is fully liable to repay the covered bonds and the cover pool assets remain on the balance sheet of the issuing bank, leaving no question around the alignment of interest between issuer and investor. For banks and non-banks with high senior unsecured credit ratings, a covered bond issuance should allow them to issue at appreciably lower rates of interest than where they would issue unsecured debt and be competitive to where they would issue securitization debt rated as high as their own rating. In Europe, we see a significant difference between the rates paid by top-tier banks on their unsecured debt versus their covered bond issuances, with covered bond debt yields being appreciably lower than unsecured debt of comparable maturity.

5) **The legislation should stipulate a specific legal framework that supersedes general insolvency law for the absolute protection of covered bond investors, consistent with the principle articulated in number 4 above.** In our view, investor reception of a US covered bond market will be directly determined by the issuer insolvency framework that accompanies it. If investors fear that an issuer's regulator, the FDIC in the case of US IDIs, can interfere with or have a claim upon the assets in a cover pool, then US covered bonds will be relatively unattractive compared to those issued in other jurisdictions where the priority of claim of bondholders on cover pool assets is a cornerstone of covered bond legislation. Investors would treat them as quasi-secured but price them more like unsecured, which in turn would eliminate the motivation for issuers to issue. If investors fear that an issuer's regulator can force the early liquidation of a covered

pool, and leave them under-secured or at risk of reinvesting par proceeds in lower-yielding investments, investors will most likely require a risk premium that would again increase the cost of issuance relative to an issuer's alternatives. Worse still, from a systemic perspective, such a covered bond paradigm would miss a great opportunity to introduce a great stabilizer in the world of bank asset-liability management. The ability to pledge assets under a robust and investor-friendly secured financing framework, like covered bonds, offers banks and non-banks alike a potentially valuable source of financing and simultaneously offers investors a safer investment during periods of credit and liquidity stress in our financial system. This benefit should not be understated and can become of paramount importance and utility during periods of heightened counterparty credit concerns, like the extreme counterparty credit concerns we experienced in the Credit Crisis of 2008. Indeed, it was precisely this potential that motivated the former US Treasury Secretary Henry Paulson to advance a covered bond framework, but the initiative came too late into the crisis and relied on a weaker regulatory approach rather than a stronger legislative approach to have counteracted the overwhelming forces we confronted in an enormous crisis that was accelerating at the time.

6) **The assets in a cover pool should be segregated from the issuer's other assets, or clearly identified as such to avoid any likelihood that cover pool assets would become co-mingled with other assets of the issuer or with an issuer's insolvency estate.** Covered bond investors should bear no doubt over the proper identification and segregation of assets comprising the cover pool which secures them. One way to assure such treatment would be to require a periodic audit of an issuer's books and records to determine that the asset segregation standard has been satisfied, to report any deficiencies to a responsible party, and to assure an actionable remedy is imposed on a capable party to cure any non-compliance in a timely fashion.

7) **The issuer should maintain a continuing obligation to "cover" the bonds issued under their covered bond program with a sufficient level of collateral and overcollateralization consisting of performing (non-defaulted), self-liquidating financial assets.** This requirement is universally incorporated into covered bond programs around the world and provides assurance to investors that the cover pool would at all times generate sufficient, self-liquidating proceeds

from performing financial assets to repay the full amount of principal and interest without their having to rely on the issuer's unsecured credit quality to do so.

8) **The maturity limit applicable to covered bonds (and cover pool assets) should extend to 30 years.** Such a limit is consistent with the FDIC's Final Policy, which was increased from 10 years after consideration of comments received on their Interim Policy Statement and the FDIC's own view that "longer-term covered bonds should not pose a significant, additional risk and may avoid short-term funding volatility."15 A 30-year term limit would allow issuers to tap into the long-end of the yield curve and better maturity-match to longer dated assets, such as 30-year, fixed-rate mortgages. With regard to such a feature, like a maturity limit on cover pool assets, the more flexibility the final legislation affords issuers, the more likely issuance will emerge.

9) **Covered bonds should be allowed to include provisions for additional credit enhancements, liquidity support, interest rate and currency swaps or options.** These types of instruments may prove useful, and even necessary, by the market to create a more stable investment profile for investors and an even better asset-liability match for issuers than they might otherwise be able to achieve if the use of hedge instruments like the ones mentioned here were disallowed or unnecessarily restricted.

OTHER CONSIDERATIONS FOR THE LEGISLATIVE PROCESS

In promoting the principles set forth above, it may also be worth noting that our members do not necessarily feel that the legislation needs to be overly prescriptive. Certain elements may be best left for the market to discover, or by Treasury as the principal covered bond regulator. One such element may be the level of overcollateralization. Considering that Dodd-Frank is mandating risk retention for asset securitization on the order of 5% generally, it should be a strikingly clear distinction that covered bonds, by definition, have a 100% risk retention associated with them. This being the case, overcollateralization would exist solely for the benefit of global, market-based investors of adequate sophistication to evaluate the appropriateness of overcollateralization requirements vis à vis the collateral comprising a cover pool. As our recommendation is to allow a wide range of collateral to be eligible for inclusion in covered bond programs, it would be natural to let the investor market set corresponding overcollateralization requirements, especially since we know from experience that different types of assets require different levels of overcollateralization to achieve comparable credit profiles for the liabilities issued against the assets. This would make sense from the regulator's perspective as well, as in theory, regulators would prefer lower overcollateralization requirements so more assets are immediately available to depositors and unsecured creditors than would otherwise be the case if overcollateralization levels were mandated at levels above what was needed in the market.

Other features of an emergent covered bond system may be best decided by legislation if it is likely regulation will only serve to restrain the formation of a deep and liquid market. For example, the FDIC Final Policy restricts covered bond issuance to 4% of an IDI's liabilities.

While their reasoning is understandable,[16] a 4% limit would impose a theoretical initial maximum market size for covered bond issuance of $474 billion, assuming the highly improbable outcome that every bank issued to their maximum limit.[17] When banks are already subject to leverage ratios, we question the necessity of requiring an initial market size cap that could merely serve to dissuade issuance by signaling to IDI's that covered bonds will not be allowed to become a sufficiently meaningful asset-liability tool needed to justify the upfront commitment of time, effort, money, and resources to commence an issuance program.

Still, other features are worthy of inclusion in any final legislation, and some may even be necessary for a US covered bond market. For example, it is typical of many European covered bond frameworks to provide for special supervision of an issuer's obligations in respect of the cover pool, which is supervision specifically for the benefit of covered bondholders, as compared to more general credit institution or markets supervision. Frequently, this kind of supervision is conducted by designated public authorities, which frequently require a covered bond issuer to obtain a license to issue covered bonds. In a number of countries, the public authority is also the banking supervisory authority. In others, the covered bond supervisory authority is the markets regulator. Such public authorities either appoint or approve a cover pool monitor to assure covenant compliance with the terms and conditions of the covered pool legal contracts, and some of these authorities may conduct their own periodic audits of the cover pool programs they supervise. Article 22 (4) of the Directive in Undertakings for Collective Investment in Transferable Securities (the "UCITS Directive"), which is included in other EC directives, affords favorable treatment, such as risk weightings, to covered bonds subject to special public supervision. Calibrating the legislation to afford special treatment for covered bond investments could enlarge the potential for this new market and may also be necessary if US covered bonds are to find as broad and deep an investor base as the covered bonds issued from frameworks in other countries.

CONCLUSION

Given the extensive history, longevity, and size of the European covered bond market and the remaining need to encourage private sector credit flows in the United States, the ASF is strongly supportive of a legislative framework for US covered bonds. Our support comes despite the potential for covered bond issuance to draw market share from securitization issuance. This is because we believe securitization will re-emerge as a healthy and viable financing, capital-management, and risk-management technology whether or not a covered bond market is established in the United States. Moreover, covered bonds and securitization can co-exist in a complementary fashion with one another, as they have for some time in Europe. We also believe it is our obligation as professionals to advocate for disciplined, market-based developments that will promote the availability and affordability of consumer credit to all Americans, just as securitization has been doing for many years. We believe that industry, legislators, regulators, and other policymakers can work in an open, democratic fashion to innovate financial solutions for this greater good. We applaud Chairman Garrett, his co-sponsor Congresswoman Maloney, and this Subcommittee for its forward-thinking initiative and persistence to see the dawn of a new financial technology that will establish a more balanced continuum of asset-liability management alternatives for our credit institutions. By offering credit institutions the ability to issue longer-term, secured liabilities, covered bonds will fill a void that exists among existing alternatives, like short-term unsecured debt (eg, demand deposits), short-term secured debt (eg, repos), longer-term unsecured debt (eg, term CDs and MTNs), and securitization. The filling of such a void can lower the cost of financing a credit institution, which in turn can lower the cost of consumer credit while simultaneously expanding its availability. At a time when we need to transfer public sector support for private sector financing back to the private sector to reduce our fiscal deficits and remove our potentially inflationary monetary policies; at a time when we need to find avenues to create and expand credit to drive consumer spending and real GDP growth; at a time when we need to create jobs, this covered bond legislation could not come at a better time for the financial industry or our economy.

Again, I thank you very much for the opportunity to testify here today and look forward to answering any questions that you may have.

End Notes

[1] Best Practices for Residential Covered Bonds, Department of the Treasury, July 2008.

[2] A framework not defined by specific legislation (a "legislative framework") is herein referred to interchangeably as a regulatory framework, policy framework, or contractual framework.

[3] "Washington Mutual's Covered Bonds", Harvard Business School, 9-209-0923, Daniel B. Bergstresser, Robin Greenwood, James Quinn, Rev. October 22, 2009.

[4] Federal Register Vo. 76, No. 38, Friday February 25, 2011, Part II, Federal Deposit Insurance Corporation, 12 CFR, Part 327, Assessments, Large Bank Pricing; Final Rule, page 10673.

[5] Ibid

[6] Statement of Michael H. Krimminger, Deputy to the Chairman, Federal Deposit Insurance Corporation on Covered Bonds: Potential Uses and Regulatory Issues, Committee on Banking, Housing, and Urban Affairs, U.S. Senate, September 15, 2010.

[7] *The Conundrum of Covered Bonds*, Steven L. Schwarcz, forthcoming in The Business Lawyer, May 2011.

[8] *Natixis Credit Research*, Cristina Costa and Jennifer Levy, March 2011.

[9] European Covered Bond Fact Book, European Covered Bond Council, September 2009.

[10] Ibid

[11] *Natixis Credit Research*, Cristina Costa and Jennifer Levy, March 2011.

[12] Ibid

[13] Ibid

[14] *Natixis Credit Research*, Spreads and Credit, Covered Bond, November 2010, Christina Costa, Jennifer Levy, in collaboration with François Le Roy.

[15] Federal Register / Vol. 73, No. 146 / Monday July 28, 2008, page 43756.

[16] "The 4 percent limitation under the Policy Statement is designed to permit the FDIC, and other regulators, an opportunity to evaluate the development of the covered bond market within the financial system of the United States, which differs in many respects from that in other countries deploying covered bonds." Federal Register / Vol. 73, No. 145 / Monday July 28, 2008, page 43756.

[17] Fitch Ratings, U.S. Housing Reform Proposal FAQs: Filling the Void, February 24, 2011

In: Covered Bonds: Features and Proposals ISBN: 978-1-61470-118-7
Editors: Wei Zhao and Chan Li © 2011 Nova Science Publishers, Inc.

Chapter 6

TESTIMONY OF STEPHEN G. ANDREWS, BANK OF ALAMEDA, BEFORE THE U.S. HOUSE SUBCOMMITTEE ON CAPITAL MARKETS AND GOVERNMENT SPONSORED ENTERPRISES, HEARING ON "LEGISLATIVE PROPOSALS TO CREATE A COVERED BOND MARKET IN THE UNITED STATES"[*]

Mr. Chairman and Ranking Member, my name is Steve Andrews. I am pleased to appear before you today at this hearing on covered bonds and the United States Covered Bond Act of 2011. This is a very important issue and I am pleased to see the thoughtfulness being shown by the Congress in studying the covered bond market.

I am a community banker with the Bank of Alameda in Alameda, California, a successful California community bank. We guard jealously our community reputation and take pride in the positive impact that we have in our communities. We are conservatively run, and we know our customers well.

I am pleased to present testimony raising several serious concerns and objections about the possible development of a covered bond market in the Un ited States (U.S.). To cut to the chase, speaking from my perspective as a

---

[*] This is an edited, reformatted and augmented version of testimony given by Stephen G. Andrews, Bank of Alameda, before the U.S. House Subcommittee on Capital Markets and Government Sponsored Enterprises, Hearing on "Legislative Proposals to Create a Covered Bond Market in the United States" on MARCH 11, 2001.

community banker, I do not think that we as a country need to expend the time, energy and resources to attempt to create a covered bond market in the U.S. In my opinion, and I believe that I am supported in this view by Treasury Secretary Geithner, wealready have a covered bond market: it is the Federal Home Loan Bank System. I am a member of the Federal Home Loan Bank of San Francisco. We do not need to try to import from Europe an experimental housing finance tool that would be deployed under greatly different conditions and circumstances and as far as I can see would largely benefit the biggest banks in the industry.

By contrast, the Federal Home Loan Bank (FHLB) system is al ive and well and doing the job congress chartered it to do. Let me remind you that the FHLB system expands and serves as a buffer to its members under its cooperative ownership structure when the economy demands it, and the system contracts when the economy no longer requires that level of liquidity. Indeed, consistent with the Federal Home Loan Bank Act, the Federal Home Loan banks provide funds in good and bad economic times. During the height of the mortgage credit crunch in 2007 -2008, Federal Home Loan banks increased their advances to member institutions by over $250 billion. Frozen out of credit markets during the financial crisis, large and small institutions relied on Federal Home Loan banks for funding. If such funding had not been available at reasonable cost, the crisis would have been even worse. In sum, Federal Home Loan banks manage mortgage collateral differently. Federal Home Loan Banks take haircuts on the collateral provided. Most importantly they know their customers and are able to customize funding needs to meet mortgage -financing needs in a way that covered bonds are not intended to achieve. Because true low risk covered bonds require term debt to match up with term assets.

I am not here to "bash" the big banks. They are an important part of the FHLB System. As members and users of that System, both large and small institutions contribute to its strengths and permit it to make reasonably priced advances which members use to make mortgages. Without large member participation, the System would not be as strong as it is and able to provide reasonably priced advances.

My understanding is that a covered bond is a recourse debt obligation of the bond issuer (usually a depository institution), in which the issuer has a continuing interest in the performance of the loan, and is secured by a pool of mortgage assets. Covered bonds provide funding to the bond issuer, and the issuer retains the pool of assets and related credit risk on its balance sheet. Therefore, in contrast to mortg age backed securities, where secured assets are off the balance sheet of the issuer, the pools of assets remain on the covered bond issuer's balance sheet.

Interest on the covered bonds are paid to investors from the issuer's general cash flows, while the pool of assets serve as secured collateral on the products.

If the assets within the covered bond's asset pool become non-performing, they should be replaced with cash or be over collateralized. The issuer must maintain a pool of assets in excess of the notional value of a covered bond and therefore be "over-collateralized" at all times. In general, the maturity of a covered bond is greater than one year and no more than thirty years; in Europe assets are matched for the durations of the covered bond. Moreover, while the majority of covered bond issuances have maturities between one and ten years, there has been a recent trend toward longer-term instruments that are greater than ten years in duration.

Unfortunately, the lion share of the benefits of a covered bond market in the U.S. would be to help the largest banks in the U.S. to the detriment of excellent community banks. Moreover, instead of the covered bond market being an effort to privatize mortgage finance obligations as is sometimes touted as a benefit, it seems pretty clear that in Europe the government is viewed as backing up the covered bonds issued by the large European banks and indeed the various governments in Europe have stepped in to support the covered bond markets when difficulties arose.

The U.S. has over 7000 banks while Germany and other European nations often have 3 or 4 major banks and a small number of additional institutions. The latter financial market structure, with fewer and larger banks, is more conducive to covered bon d issuances. Smaller community banks would be at a competitive disadvantage in a covered bond market because they do not have the volume of mortgages necessary to support covered bond financing. To create covered bond assets with enough diversity would require adequate "mortgage deal flow." Smaller banks in this struggling market may simply not have the number of loans to provide competitively priced covered bonds. The government or market might be able to consolidate mortgage loans for smaller banks into covered bonds, but even this solution is likely to be at a higher cost compared to larger national originators with substantial deal flow. In contrast to the U.S., European countries have different banking structures.

In addition, I believe manylower and middle-income consumers would be affected byhigher priced mortgages from small banks unable to compete with large bank issuers of covered bonds. Moreover, some contend that covered bonds will include mortgages with down payments of 20% or more and because of duration matching, may encourage mortgages of less than 30 years. Such a result would obviously not be in the best interests of consumers or small banks that serve them.

Moreover, the Federal Deposit Insurance Corporation (FDIC) has raised serious concerns about the functioning of a covered bond market and the ability of the FDIC to resolve financial institutions that fail which hold such instruments. The FDIC's 2008 Final Statement of Policy on Covered Bonds (FDIC Policy Statement) is the pertinent position of the FDIC on the use of covered bonds. One of the main concerns detailed in the FDIC Policy Statement was the potential for covered bonds to increase the costs to the FDIC's deposit insurance fund in a receivership. More specific ally, the FDIC was concerned that unrestricted growth in the covered bond market could excessively increase the proportion of secured liabilities to unsecured liabilities, which could lead to a smaller value of assets that are available to satisfy depositors and creditors in a receivership and therefore lead to a greater potential loss for the FDIC's deposit insurance fund. The FDIC is also concerned about the agency's potential inability to obtain proceeds from covered bonds in the insolvency process in circumstances when the covered bond issuer has failed. The FDIC also stated its concern about being powerless to repudiate covered bond contracts in the insolvency process which could transfer risk from covered bond investors to the general public.

Some argue that the bill would allow covered bonds to be removed from the FDIC Insurance coverage. If this were the case, it would lower the amount of insurance that large institutions pay into the FDIC fund and potentially increase the cost of FDIC insurance on small community banks.

As to the proposed bill, as drafted, it contains provisions that some argue could have far reaching implications. Namely, expanding covered bonds to include other forms of collateral beyond mortgages, using assets as substitute collateral instead of cash and potential providing a federal guarantee to covered bond-issuing entities – namely large banks.

As to the proposed bill, as drafted, it contains provisions that could have far reaching implications namely expanding covered bonds to include other forms of collateral beyond mortgages, using assets as substitute collateral rather than cash, and potentially providing a federal guarantee to covered bond-issuing entities – namely large banks.

1) The Act would allow for covered bond usage on non-mortgage assets that have short duration such as credit cards, auto loans, and student loans. This is the opposite of the established European model.

Testimony of Stephen G. Andrews ... 99

2) The legislation also refers to dynamic collateral, which can mean that a large bank does not have to buy the non-performing asset out with cash, which could be problematic. Dynamic capital was the equivalent of what WAMU did when it issued covered bonds, and substituted loans internally rather than providing cash, and we all know what happened to WAMU.

3) The legislation also request that a study be performed on how the government could provide a backstop to the covered bond market. If a backstop is put in place, large lenders could have a government guarantee in a way that could be riskier and more expansive than Fannie Mae or Freddie Mac.

Now, as a country, we should have a robust debate about the level of home ownership in the U.S. And, I will be the first to admit that banks and others made mistakes during the housing bubble and ensuing recession by too aggressively pushing marginal borrowers into home ownership. But, let's be clear. Owning a home is a vital part of the American dream. In Germany and other European nations that rely on the restrictive processes of the covered bond market, the national home ownership rate is below 50%. That's not part of the American fabric or part of our culture. Americans want to be able to work hard, save a reasonable amount of money for a down payment and own their "castle," and have the freedom to move elsewhere in this great country if employment, family or other obligations requires a change in residence. That's not the way it works with covered bonds. Borrowers are locked in by the onerous down payment, underwriting criteria and inability to sell and relocate to another residence for whatever reason of personal freedom or economic necessity. Having the personal freedom to move where you want and to play by the rules to grab your piece of the American dream, well that's the America that I grew up in. That's the country that I am proud of, and that's what is fair to keep in place for my children, your children, my grandchildren, your grandchildren and the other generations in the years ahead.

Let me close with this thought. Housing should be viewed as a long term investment and as a place of belonging. It should not be transformed through legislation or other marketplace maneuvering into a financial speculative asset. That happened during the financial crisis and the housing bubble that contributed mightily to that crisis. I suggest that you consider some principlesto guide any covered bond legislation such as; (1) do no harm to the 30 year mortgage as the industry standard; (2) insure a robust Federal Home Loan Bank System that provides a significant advance product to large, medium and small banks at a reasonable cost; (3) not increase FDIC insurance fees on smaller banks as a consequence of establishing a covered bond market; and (4) ensure consumers are held harmless in their continual search for low interest and nationally available mortgages.

I thank you for the opportunity to appear before you today, and I welcome the opportunity to respond to your questions.

In: Covered Bonds: Features and Proposals ISBN: 978-1-61470-118-7
Editors: Wei Zhao and Chan Li © 2011 Nova Science Publishers, Inc.

Chapter 7

STATEMENT OF THE FEDERAL DEPOSIT INSURANCE CORPORATION, BEFORE THE U.S. HOUSE SUBCOMMITTEE ON CAPITAL MARKETS AND GOVERNMENT SPONSORED ENTERPRISES, HEARING ON "LEGISLATIVE PROPOSALS TO CREATE A COVERED BOND MARKET IN THE UNITED STATES"[*]

The FDIC appreciates the opportunity to provide its views on the regulatory and legislative issues posed by covered bonds. The FDIC has long worked with the financial industry to establish a sound foundation for a vibrant covered bond market that will provide U.S. banks with an additional source of liquidity. These efforts include working with the first U.S. banks to issue covered bonds in 2006 and the FDIC's adoption in July 2008, of a Statement of Policy on the treatment of covered bonds to clarify key issues related to deposit insurance and bank resolutions. Our efforts facilitated the creation of a market-tested and market-accepted covered bond program for U.S. banks that meets investors' needs without increasing the government's exposure to this investment class.

---

[*] This is an edited, reformatted and augmented version of testimony given by Federal Deposit Insurance Corporation, before the U.S. House Subcommittee on Capital Markets and Government Sponsored Enterprises, Hearing on "Legislative Proposals to Create a Covered Bond Market in the United States" on March 11, 2011.

102 Statement of the Federal Deposit Insurance Corporation

The FDIC has significant concerns with the proposed legislation, the *United States Covered Bond Act of 2011" (H.R. 290)*. The FDIC believes that this legislation fails to maintain that important balance between investor demands and government exposure, providing investors with lopsided benefits at the direct expense of the Deposit Insurance Fund (DIF).

As discussed in more detail below, the regime set up in H.R. 940 creates an implied subsidy to financial institutions and investors that does not exist for any other privately issued security. The bill provides for a new class of investments that is "risk free" by giving covered bond investors protections in the form of an unfettered claim on significant amounts of collateral that would be unavailable to any other creditors, including the FDIC. This structure will skew the market, limit the demand for long-term, stable unsecured debt, and will thwart the nascent efforts to enhance market discipline in the wake of the financial crisis. At a time when the government is carefully removing its extraordinary support of the financial system, we should not create a new permanent government subsidy of the financial markets.

The FDIC believes this legislation will create winners and losers. The creation of this new government program will primarily benefit large complex financial institutions which already enjoy funding advantages over smaller financial institutions and nonfinancial commercial entities of all sizes. To provide these firms with additional government backed funding advantages over smaller banks and nonfinancial firms would be at odds with everything we learned coming out of the crisis and work in contravention to current efforts to end too big to fail. Since covered bonds are likely to be issued by only the largest FDIC insured institutions, their failure would pose a risk of substantial losses to the DIF. Moreover, given the likely limited number of issuers, it would not be practical for such losses to be absorbed solely by the other covered bond issuers. This shifting of risk from investors to the FDIC as deposit insurer is unacceptable in our view.

The FDIC believes that the legislation fails to recognize that U.S. banks already have access to a covered bond market – one that was able to grow without the need for a government guarantee. Covered bonds were successfully issued prior to the 2008 crisis, and in fact, the FDIC was able to sell an intact covered bond program from a receivership of a failed thrift.

The FDIC believes that the existing U.S. covered bond market has significant advantages over the European model from a taxpayer perspective. European programs offer generous collateral protections to investors, and as a result, trade more like sovereign debt than bank or securitization debt. One of the clear lessons of the financial crisis is that such government guarantees or

Statement of the Federal Deposit Insurance Corporation ... 103

subsidies can distort normal market prices by essentially providing 'risk-free' investments. We have already seen the devastating consequences when risks are mispriced in the market.

Further, the independent financial regulatory agencies are experienced safety and soundness supervisors and standards setters - yet do not have a leading role under H.R. 940 in setting safety and soundness standards for the prudent development and operation of a covered bond market. The types of assets employed to support a covered bond can have an impact on the overall performance of the issuer (an insured depository institution).

This statement will provide background on covered bonds, discuss the FDIC's principles for a covered bond program outlined above, and address the proposed legislation, H.R. 940.

COVERED BONDS IN CONTEXT

Covered bonds are general obligation bonds of the issuer, normally an insured bank or thrift, with payment secured by a pledge of a pool of loans. During normal operations, like any general obligation corporate bond, investors are paid from the issuing bank's general cash flows, while the cover pool of loans serves simply as collateral for the bank's duty to pay the investors. As a result, both functionally and legally, the cover pool is not the source for repayment, as in a securitization, but is simply collateral to secure payment if the issuing bank cannot make payment from its general cash flows.

Another distinction between covered bonds and most securitizations further demonstrates that the cover pools function as collateral and not as sources of payment when covered bonds are not in default. In a covered bond, any loans and other assets in the cover pool that become delinquent must be replaced with performing assets. As a result, the collateral for the covered bond is constantly refreshed—and the issuing bank has an ongoing obligation to produce new loans or other qualifying collateral to replace delinquencies. Finally, the issuer must always maintain more collateral in the cover pool than the outstanding notional or "face" balance of the outstanding bonds. If the issuing bank fails to pay on the covered bond, then the investors have recourse to the cover pool as secured creditors. This is precisely how normal collateral arrangements work in other secured transactions.

Under the long-standing U.S. law applied to all types of secured transactions, secured creditors have a claim to the collateral—here the loans or other assets pledged to secure payment on the covered bond—only to the full

104   Statement of the Federal Deposit Insurance Corporation

amount of their claim for payment at the time of any default. They do not have a claim to any part of the value of the collateral that exceeds their current claim for payment. Any collateral or proceeds in excess of that claim for payment are returned to the debtor or, if it has been placed into bankruptcy or receivership, are used to pay the claims of unsecured creditors. If, on the other hand, the secured creditor's claims are greater than the value of the collateral, the creditor will have a secured claim up to the value of the collateral and an unsecured, general claim for the remaining balance along with other unsecured creditors.

The same rules apply in FDIC receiverships. Secured creditors are fully protected under Section 11(e)(12) of the Federal Deposit Insurance Act ("FDI Act") for the amount of their claim up to the value of the collateral. As a result, covered bonds provide two avenues for recovery—from the issuing bank and from the cover pool of collateral. What they do not have, and should not have, under U.S. law, is a right to keep collateral in excess of their right to payment.

LEGISLATION TO ADDRESS COVERED BONDS

As mentioned at the outset, the FDIC supports balanced covered bond legislation. However, any such legislation should avoid transferring investment risks to the public sector or to the DIF and should remain consistent with long-standing U.S. law and policy for secured creditors. Unfortunately, H.R. 940 would muddy the relationship between investors and regulators, transfer some of the investment risks to the public sector and the DIF, and provide covered bond investors with rights that no other creditors have in a bank receivership. As a result, this legislation could lead to increased losses in failed banks that have issued covered bonds.

THE UNITED STATES COVERED BOND ACT OF 2011

H.R. 940, the *United States Covered Bond Act of 2011*, establishes new standards for the development of a covered bond market in the U.S. It requires the Secretary of the Treasury ("Treasury") to establish an oversight program that would prescribe minimum overcollateralization requirements, identify eligible asset classes for cover pools, and create a registry to enhance the transparency of covered bond programs. The banking agencies would carry out the Treasury-prescribed oversight program. A critical portion of the bill deals with an issuer's default on its covered bond obligations, and the procedure for dealing with the covered bond program of an issuer in receivership. The bill calls for the transfer of the assets of the pools securing the covered bonds out of the receivership estate and into a separate estate solely for the benefit of the covered bond investors. Upon a joint determination by the Secretary and the FDIC that the DIF suffered losses because of the resolution of the covered bonds through the separate estates, the FDIC may recover such losses by assessments on other covered bond issuers.

LEGISLATION SHOULD NOT CREATE A NEW SUBSIDY FOR COVERED BOND INVESTORS

As stated earlier, no new government program should create an implied subsidy or guarantee for financial institutions or investors. A new class of investments that appears "risk free" by providing covered bond investors with protections unavailable for any other creditors will skew the market and lead to moral hazard.

If, as proposed in the bill, the investors are secured by the entire cover pool for the duration of the covered bonds irrespective of the degree of over-collateralization, it will provide a strong incentive for investors to maximize the over-collateralization. Naturally, this will increase pressure on the issuing bank during periods of stress. The creation of separate estates consisting of the entire cover pool will also further reduce the loan assets available for sale by the FDIC in any receivership. If creditors of covered bonds are shielded from all risks, there is a strong possibility that covered bonds could lead to a mispricing of risk and distortions in the market, imperiling banks in the future. On the other hand, if the long-standing treatment of secured creditors is maintained – which would allow the FDIC to pay the outstanding principal and interest on the bonds and recover the over-collateralization—there will be very limited incentive for the creditors to demand increasing levels of collateral as a bank becomes troubled.

The super-priority given covered bond investors by the proposed bill also runs against the policy direction established by Congress in recent legislation. In 2005, Congress enacted Section 11(e)(13)(C) of the FDI Act, which prohibits secured creditors from exercising any rights against any property of a

106   Statement of the Federal Deposit Insurance Corporation

failed insured depository institution without the receiver's consent for the first 90 days of a bank receivership. This provision prevents secured creditors from taking and selling bank assets at fire sale prices to the detriment of the receiver and the DIF. More recently, section 215 of the Dodd-Frank Wall Street Reform and Consumer Protection Act mandates a study to evaluate whether a potential haircut on secured creditors could improve market discipline and reduce cost to the taxpayers. This study was prompted by the recognized roles that the run on secured credit and the insatiable demand for more collateral had in the financial crisis of 2008. In contrast, the unprecedented protection in the bill for one form of secured creditors— covered bond investors—runs counter to the policies underlying these provisions.

A further concern created by the proposed legislation is that it could encourage covered bond transactions that include "triggers" for early termination or default before a bank is closed by the regulators. Under the proposed bill, a separate estate, which removes the entire cover pool from the bank's control, is created upon any event of default. Once created, the separate estate and all collateral in the cover pool would be outside the control of the FDIC, as receiver for the bank. The residual value of the pool, and all of the loans, would be outside the receivership and be lost for all other creditors of the failed bank. This additional special protection creates a strong incentive for covered bond transactions to include a trigger that acts before the bank is placed into receivership. Since such a trigger would deprive the bank of the cash flows from the cover pool and signal to the market its imminent demise, the bank would almost inevitably suffer a liquidity failure. As a result, these early triggers represent another source of increased loss to the DIF.

The shift in H.R. 940 of federal regulation towards protection of the investment interest of specific investors raises significant questions about the proper role of federal regulation for individual investment programs. Issues involving investor protection are best resolved by private contracts based on transparent disclosures about the operations of covered bond programs.

In addition, the proposed bill would also make the Federal prudential regulators the appointing and supervising authority of trustees that would operate the separate estates of the covered bonds. This level of government entanglement in what are private contractual matters could also lead to an implied guarantee of covered bonds. An implied guarantee of covered bonds would put covered bonds on a near par with the government sponsored enterprises—a status that should not be granted without strong policy reasons because of the risk that status represents for taxpayers. It would also make the FDIC a virtual guarantor to covered bond investors.

An FDIC Guarantee is Not Necessary for a Successful Covered Bond Market

Any covered bond legislation must preserve the flexibility that current law provides to the FDIC in resolving failed banks—including the options of continuing to perform under the covered bond program pending a sale of the program to another bank, turn-over of the collateral to the investors, and repudiation—a statutory termination of the contracts—of the covered bond obligation. Repudiation is the authority, granted to the FDIC by Congress, to terminate (or breach) a contract and then pay statutorily-defined damages to the other parties. In the case of covered bonds, repudiation allows the FDIC, as receiver for the failed issuer, to cut-off future claims and end the obligation to replenish the cover pool with new assets. Under the FDI Act, the FDIC will then pay damages to compensate the covered bond investors.

Covered bond investors, as noted above, are secured creditors of the bank. The amount of their claim is defined by the balance or par value of outstanding bonds plus interest. The FDIC would support covered bond legislation that clarifies the amount of repudiation damages to be the par value of outstanding bonds plus interest accrued through the date of payment. This provides a remedy that fully reimburses the covered bond investors. In return, as in any other repudiation, the FDIC as receiver would be entitled to reclaim the collateral in the cover pool after payment of those damages. The receiver could then sell this collateral and use the proceeds to satisfy the claim of the DIF (which has the largest receivership claim as a result of having satisfied its insurance obligation for insured deposits), uninsured depositors, and other creditors of the failed bank.

If the FDIC does not repudiate a covered bond, it should have the authority to continue to perform under the covered bond until it can sell the program to another bank, as it did with WAMU's covered bonds. This strategy would not expose the investors to any loss, by definition, since the FDIC would meet all requirements of the covered bond program, including replenishment of the cover pool and meeting the overcollateralization requirement. As long as the FDIC is performing under a covered bond agreement, covered bond legislation should not limit the time in which the FDIC has to decide how best to proceed.

Any legislation that fails to preserve these important receivership authorities would make the FDIC the *de facto* guarantor of covered bonds and the *de facto* insurer of covered bond investors.

108   Statement of the Federal Deposit Insurance Corporation

We saw the beginnings of a covered bond market develop in the U.S. without such a government guarantee. Before the crisis, the FDIC worked closely with Washington Mutual Bank and Bank of America when they launched the first U.S. covered bond programs in 2006. As a result of our efforts, the banks were able to issue covered bonds at a competitive price. The 2008 Statement of Policy adopted by the FDIC's Board of Directors addressed questions from the marketplace about how covered bonds would be treated in the receivership of an issuing bank. The market's reaction to this Statement was very positive, and most commentators stated that it provided a solid foundation for the covered bond market. Shortly after the adoption of the Statement of Policy, the Department of the Treasury ("Treasury") issued a companion document entitled "Best Practices for Residential Covered Bonds" to establish greater clarity and homogeneity for the market so that investors would have confidence in future issuances. The FDIC worked with the Treasury in developing the Best Practices to create a coordinated framework for the responsible and measured roll-out and further development of covered bonds in the U.S. With the FDIC and Treasury guidance, we have seen the successful launch of a covered bond market in the Unites States that does not require implicit government guarantees. This is in contrast to developments in Europe where there do appear to be implicit government guarantees, as we noted above.

Given the FDIC's existing Statement of Policy, the Treasury's companion Best Practices, and the prior successful covered bond programs developed in cooperation with the FDIC, it is unclear that legislation is necessary to re-launch the market. At a minimum, the FDIC suggests that its Statement of Policy should be considered as a framework for any legislation in order to provide a sound, balanced foundation for the market.

TREASURY SHOULD NOT SET SAFETY AND SOUNDNESS REQUIREMENTS

Another concern with the proposed legislation is that it assigns Treasury the responsibility to set standards for the covered bond oversight program. Any legislation establishing a regulatory framework for covered bonds should instead require the appropriate federal banking regulators to establish joint standards for covered bond issuances by regulated institutions. The oversight program contemplated in H.R. 940 is essentially designed to set safety and

Statement of the Federal Deposit Insurance Corporation ... 109

soundness standards, and as such, is more appropriately the province of the prudential regulators. Moreover, such an allocation of responsibility would violate the longstanding principle of federal bank regulators having independence from the Treasury in establishing prudential banking policies for insured depository institutions ("IDIs"). This is especially important for the FDIC, as insurer and receiver, since never in our nearly eight decades of FDIC independence has the Treasury interfered with our resolution and assessment mechanism.

The resulting standards, like the FDIC's Statement of Policy, should address the key elements in covered bond transactions and the safety and soundness issues that can be implicated by a bank's use of covered bonds. The banking regulators, working in concert, should address the types of collateral, underwriting standards, required overcollateralization, frequency and content of reports on collateral and satisfaction of required over-collateralization, disclosure standards for performance of underlying loans or assets, and the rights of the investors in the event of default. A particularly important element in the clarification of investors' rights is the treatment of the covered bonds if the issuer defaults on its payments under the bonds. This is both critical to the investor and to maintaining the balance of risks retained by the investor or transferred to other parties.

The standards setters for covered bonds should have discretion in expanding the use of covered bonds and categories of cover pool assets as sustainable markets develop and the liquidity of the instruments increases. The gradual expansion of cover pool categories is essential to ensure the quality of covered bonds and of the assets in the cover pools.

LEGISLATION SHOULD NOT INCREASE THE POTENTIAL LOSS TO THE DIF

Any covered bond legislation should not limit the FDIC's ability to recover the losses the DIF incurs in resolving a failed bank. The proposed legislation would create separate estates for covered bonds if the issuer is placed in an FDIC receivership, thus removing the cover pool assets from the receivership and potentially increasing losses to the DIF. Depleting a receivership estate in this way could pose a genuine threat to the DIF.

The lack of access to the collateral over the life of the covered bonds could result in higher DIF losses and a lower DIF net worth than otherwise in

110   Statement of the Federal Deposit Insurance Corporation

many circumstances. The net worth of the DIF, as subrogee of the insured depositors and thus with the largest claim on the receivership estate, could be lowered if the receiver has to hold the residual interest in the collateral on its balance sheet at less than expected recovery value because of the residual's lack of liquidity. Additionally, the DIF net worth would be lower if the FDIC receives a lower bid for the failed covered bond issuer because of its inability to free up collateral and package the failed institution's assets in a way that would result in a resolution least costly to the DIF. This increases the chances in a period of banking turmoil that the FDIC would be forced to borrow from the entire banking industry or from the Treasury, simply because of the extraordinary protection accorded to covered bond investors under the proposed legislation.

Unfortunately, the proposed *United States Covered Bond Act of 2011* would expose the DIF to additional losses by restricting the FDIC's ability to maximize recoveries on failed bank operations and assets. This result is contrary to a long-standing Congressional goal of preserving the DIF to help maintain confidence in the U.S. banking system. Over the past several decades, Congress has revised the laws governing the resolution of failed banks on several occasions. Two of those revisions are crucial to the present discussion. First, Congress required the FDIC to use the "least costly" transaction for resolving insured depository institutions. Second, Congress created depositor preference, which gives depositors a priority superior to general unsecured creditors. Both reforms were designed to reduce losses to the DIF.

The proposed bill would restrict the FDIC's current receivership authorities used to maximize the value of the failed bank's covered bonds. The bill leaves the FDIC with only two options: continue to perform until the covered bond program is transferred to another institution within a certain timeframe, or hand over the collateral to a separate trustee for the covered bond estate, in return for a residual certificate of questionable value.

The restrictions discussed above would impair the FDIC's ability to accomplish the "least costly" resolution and could increase losses to the DIF by providing covered bond investors with a super-priority that exceeds that provided to other secured creditors. The proposed bill attempts to alleviate this problem by permitting the FDIC, upon a joint determination of loss with Treasury, to assess IDIs with covered bond programs for losses associated with the use of separate estates for covered bonds. The FDIC alone is in the best position to determine losses to the DIF as it has done for nearly 8 decades. Never in the history of the FDIC has the political branch been involved in our

Statement of the Federal Deposit Insurance Corporation ...   111

assessment mechanism. The FDI Act specifically protects the FDIC from such interference. In addition, the approach of H.R. 940 is unsound for two other reasons. First, it is likely that any covered bond issuances will be concentrated in very few, large institutions—certainly for an extended period. This concentration would, in turn, mean that any assessment to allow the DIF to recoup its losses would fall heavily on only a very few large IDIs. Indeed, the attempt to make up for such losses through assessments could threaten the stability of the remaining participating IDIs. Second, in case of a large losses that cannot be absorbed by IDIs issuing covered bonds, DIF losses would be borne by all of the more than 7,600 FDIC-insured institutions, whether or not they issued covered bonds.

The protections to the insurance fund, depositors and the flexibility afforded the FDIC as receiver of a failed depository institution has become a standard that other countries want to emulate. The flexibility that Congress afforded the FDIC permits it to respond to market conditions at the time of insolvency and to achieve bank resolutions that protect insured depositors at the least cost to the DIF. This is an important public policy that we believe has served the nation well and should be maintained.

CONCLUSION

The FDIC supports a vibrant covered bond market that would increase liquidity to financial institutions and enable sustainable and robust asset origination. However, any legislation should avoid promoting development of a covered bond market that provides for zero risk to covered bond investors and gives rights to investors that are superior to any other secured creditor – thus reducing market discipline and protection for the DIF. Further – and just as important – the banking regulators, and not the Treasury, should be the lead in promulgating safety and soundness regulations for insured depository institutions involved in the covered bond market. We believe the principles described above will ensure that covered bonds serve as a viable investment for bondholders and the financial system. We will continue to work with the Congress, other regulators and market participants on ways to create a sustainable covered bond market in the U.S.

In: Covered Bonds: Features and Proposals
Editors: Wei Zhao and Chan Li

ISBN: 978-1-61470-118-7
© 2011 Nova Science Publishers, Inc.

Chapter 8

BEST PRACTICES FOR RESIDENTIAL COVERED BONDS[*]

The Department of the Treasury

Henry M. Paulson, Jr.
Secretary of the Treasury

I. BACKGROUND

This Best Practices guide has been prepared by the Department of the Treasury ("Treasury") in order to encourage the growth of the Covered Bond market in the United States. Treasury believes that Covered Bonds represent a potential additional source of financing that could reduce borrowing costs for homeowners, improve liquidity in the residential mortgage market, and help depository institutions strengthen their balance sheets by diversifying their funding sources.

U.S. depository institutions have historically utilized several different funding sources to originate new residential mortgage loans, both for sale to investors and for their own portfolios. For loans sold into the market, depository institutions' funding options included selling the loans directly to

---

[*] This is an edited, reformatted and augmented version of The Department of the Treasury publication, dated July 2008.

investors, Fannie Mae, or Freddie Mac, and via private-label securitization. For loans retained on their balance sheets, depository institutions' funding options included utilizing their customers' deposits, issuing unsecured debt, and pledging their mortgages as collateral for advances from the Federal Home Loan Banks.

Recent market turmoil has severely limited the ability of depository institutions to sell loans to investors via private-label securitization. Consistent with their important public policy mission, the government-sponsored enterprises, Fannie Mae, Freddie Mac and the Federal Home Loans Banks, as well as the Federal Housing Administration have been playing a critical role by providing mortgage finance during this strained period. Even so, many depository institutions are keeping more mortgage loans on their balance sheets and are therefore seeking new sources of on-balance sheet financing. Many U.S. depository institutions are examining the potential of Covered Bonds to provide this financing while at the same time diversifying their overall funding portfolio.

Private-label securitization has become strained. The GSEs, FHA and balance sheet lending have expanded in response. Nonetheless, total mortgage originations have fallen.

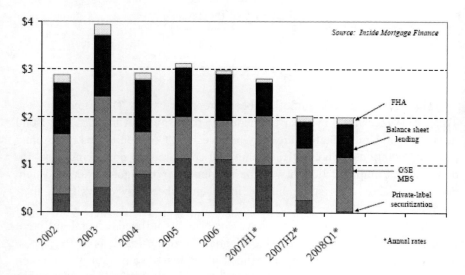

Mortgage Originations by Source of Funding (trillions of dollars).

The Federal Home Loan Banks are playing an important and expanded role funding lenders' balance sheets.

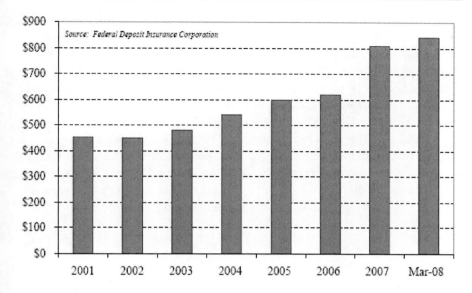

Federal Home Loan Bank Advances (billions of dollars outstanding, end of period).

Even with the expanded roles of Fannie Mae, Freddie Mac, the Federal Home Loan Banks and the Federal Housing Administration, mortgage spreads are increasing for all classes of mortgage loans.

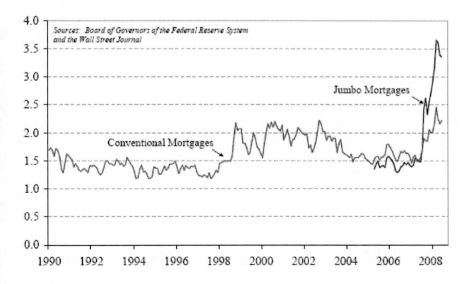

Mortgage Rate Spreads to 10-Year Treasury (percent).

116 The Department of the Treasury

Covered Bonds present an alternative source of funding for institutions that can complement other sources of financing for a wide range of high-quality assets. In Europe, Covered Bonds are highly liquid instruments which are typically sold to rate-product investors rather than credit-product investors. While a Covered Bond market is already well-established in Europe, to date only two U.S. depository institutions have issued Covered Bonds. Given current challenges in other financing markets, U.S. institutions may find Covered Bonds to be an attractive source of funding for mortgage loans.

Treasury expects private-label securitization to return to the U.S. mortgage market, enabling homeowners to benefit from a broad, global investor base. Given the size of the U.S. residential mortgage market, Treasury believes there will be a role for all sources of mortgage funding in the future.

II. OBJECTIVE

In preparing this report, Treasury seeks to bring increased clarity and homogeneity to the United States Covered Bond market by developing a series of Best Practices. Although the United States does not have dedicated Covered Bond legislation, Treasury believes these Best Practices may serve as a starting-point for the market, by encouraging issuers to use a common and simplified structure with high quality collateral for Covered Bond issuances. However, this document does not imply that Treasury favors Covered Bonds over other financing options available to depository institutions. Instead, Treasury views Covered Bonds as an additional, complementary funding source for the $11 trillion residential mortgage market.

Treasury has limited these Best Practices specifically to Covered Bonds backed by collateral consisting of high quality residential mortgage loans for two reasons. First, a liquid Covered Bond market based on residential mortgages may provide additional funding for the housing market, in turn lowering mortgage rates for homeowners. Second, focusing on one type of collateral while the market is nascent will provide simplicity for market participants. However, Treasury expects that the Covered Bond market to develop over time and the collateral securing Covered Bonds may eventually include other asset classes.

It should be noted that these Best Practices serve as a complement to the Federal Deposit Insurance Corporation's *Final Covered Bond Policy Statement* dated July 15, 2008 (see Appendix B). This statement specifies actions that the FDIC will take during an insolvency or receivership if the Covered Bond meets certain minimum requirements.

Finally, while these Best Practices have been developed to facilitate the growth of the Covered Bond market, they should not constrain the market in the future. Treasury fully expects the structure, collateral and other key terms of Covered Bonds to evolve with the growth of this market in the United States.

In preparing this Best Practices document, Treasury discussed the potential development of the U.S. Covered Bond market with both U.S. and European regulators, as well as numerous market participants, including potential issuers, investors, underwriters, rating agencies, law firms, financial counterparties, service providers and trade associations.

III. COVERED BOND DEFINITION

For the purposes of this document, a Covered Bond is defined as follows:

A Covered Bond is a debt instrument secured by a perfected security interest in a specific pool of collateral ("Cover Pool"). A Covered Bond provides funding to a depository institution ("issuer") that retains a Cover Pool of residential mortgage assets and related credit risk on its balance sheet. Interest on the Covered Bond is paid to investors from the issuer's general cash flows, while the Cover Pool serves as secured collateral. This Cover Pool consists of a portfolio of performing residential mortgage loans that meet specified underwriting criteria and are actively managed by the issuer to meet certain characteristics. If assets within the Cover Pool become non-performing, they must be replaced with performing assets. Finally, the issuer must maintain a Cover Pool in excess of the notional value of the Covered Bond ("overcollateralization") at all times. Multiple issuances for a depository institution may utilize a common Cover Pool.

In the event of an issuer default, Covered Bond investors first have recourse to the Cover Pool. In the event the Cover Pool returns less than par in liquidation, investors retain an unsecured claim on the issuer ranking pari passu with other unsecured creditors. Hence, Covered Bonds provide dual recourse to both the Cover Pool and the issuer, and the overcollateralization of the Cover Pool helps to mitigate the risk that investors would receive less than par in the event of an issuer default.

Comparison to Unsecured Debt

Unsecured debt differs significantly from Covered Bonds because of the absence of secured collateral underlying the obligation of the issuer. While unsecured debt investors retain an unsecured claim on the issuer in the event of issuer default, Covered Bond investors possess dual recourse to both the underlying collateral of a Covered Bond and to the individual issuer. Accordingly, Covered Bonds provide investors with additional protection on their investment compared with unsecured debt.

Comparison to Mortgage-Backed Securities

Although both mortgage-backed securities ("MBS") and Covered Bonds are a potential source of long-term funding for residential mortgage loans, there are several essential differences between Covered Bonds and MBS that make each attractive to different types of investors:

- Mortgages that secure a Covered Bond remain on the issuer's balance sheet, unlike MBS where mortgages are packaged and sold to investors.
- The cash flow from the mortgages and credit enhancements in MBS are generally the only source of principal and interest payments to the MBS investors. In a Covered Bond, principal and interest are paid by the issuer's cash flows, while the mortgages in the Cover Pool only serve as collateral for investors.
- The collateral underlying Covered Bonds is dynamic and non-performing (or prepaying) assets within the Cover Pool must be substituted with performing mortgages. Mortgages underlying MBS are static and remain in each MBS until maturity.
- In the case of an issuer default, Covered Bonds are structured to avoid prepayment prior to the date of maturity. This is accomplished through swap agreements and deposit agreements (e.g., guaranteed investment contracts). MBS investors, in contrast, are exposed to prepayment risk in the case of a mortgage default or prepayment.
- In the event that the Covered Bonds do accelerate and repay investors at an amount less than the principal and accrued interest, investors retain an unsecured claim on the issuer. MBS investors generally do

not retain any claim on the issuer in the event of repayment at an amount less than the principal and interest owed.

IV. HISTORY OF THE COVERED BOND MARKET

The Covered Bond market has a long and extensive history in Europe, dating back more than 230 years to the initial Prussian issuance in 1770. Covered Bonds were initially used to finance agriculture and later became focused on residential and commercial real estate markets. While Covered Bonds remained popular throughout the 19th century, during the 20th century they were somewhat eclipsed given other advances in the inter-bank financing markets. However, in 1995 the first German jumbo Covered Bond was issued, meeting investor demand for increasingly liquid products.[1] Since that time, the Covered Bond market has accelerated in Europe, partly due to the fact that Europe does not have government-sponsored enterprises such as Fannie Mae, Freddie Mac or the Federal Home Loan Banks. Furthermore, the collateral behind European Covered Bonds includes residential and commercial mortgages as well as public sector debt. At the end of 2007, the Covered Bond market stood at over EUR 2.11 trillion.[2] To date, two U.S. institutions have issued Covered Bonds.

Nearly all European countries have adopted Covered Bonds into their financial system. Depending on the jurisdiction, Covered Bonds may be governed by legislation (i.e. a "legislative framework") or by contract (i.e. a "structured framework"). Typically, a legislative framework exists in nations with a long history of Covered Bonds while nations with a relatively young Covered Bond market, such as Canada and Japan have a structured framework. In countries with a legislative framework there is often a dedicated regulator that governs the issuance and repayment of Covered Bonds. Moreover, a legislative framework helps to standardize Covered Bonds, providing homogeneity and simplicity to the market. This Best Practices document seeks to offer such structure to the U.S. market.

V. IMPORTANT CONSIDERATIONS

The purpose of this document is to present a standardized model for Covered Bonds issued in the United States in the absence of dedicated legislation. Investors should recognize that like all investments, Covered Bonds carry risk. Investors should perform their own due diligence and review risk factors and associated disclosure before investing in any Covered Bond. These Best Practices only serve as a template for market participants and do not in any way provide or imply a government guarantee of any kind. It should also be understood that these Best Practices do not attempt to address requirements arising from federal securities laws or any other legal framework.

VI. Best Practices Template

For a Covered Bond program to be consistent with this Best Practices Template, the program's documentation must conform to the following provisions throughout the life of the program, not only at the time of issuance. *Italics indicate provisions that are specified in the final FDIC policy statement[3].*

Issuer - The issuer may be:
- A newly created, bankruptcy-remote SPV ("SPV Structure")[4]
- A depository institution and/or a wholly-owned subsidiary of a depository institution ("Direct Issuance Structure")

Security - Under the current SPV Structure, the issuer's primary assets must be a mortgage bond purchased from a depository institution. The mortgage bond must be secured at the depository institution by a dynamic pool of residential mortgages.

Under the Direct Issuance Structure, the issuing institution must designate a Cover Pool of residential mortgages as the collateral for the Covered Bond, which remains on the balance sheet of the depository institution.

In both structures, the Cover Pool must be owned by the depository institution. Issuers of Covered Bonds must provide a first priority claim on the assets in the Cover Pool to bond holders, and the assets in the Cover Pool must not be encumbered by any other lien. The issuer must clearly identify the Cover Pool's assets, liabilities, and security pledge on its books and records.

Maturity - *The maturity for Covered Bonds shall be greater than one*

Best Practices for Residential Covered Bonds

year and no more than thirty years. While the majority of early issuances will likely have maturities between one and ten years, we expect longer dated issuances may develop over time.

Eligible Cover Pool Collateral - The collateral in the Cover Pool must meet the following requirements at all times:

- Performing mortgages on one-to-four family residential properties
- Mortgages shall be underwritten at the fully-indexed rate[5]
- Mortgages shall be underwritten with documented income
- Mortgages must comply with existing supervisory guidance governing the underwriting of residential mortgages, including the Interagency Guidance on Non-Traditional Mortgage Products, October 5, 2006, and the Interagency Statement on Subprime Mortgage Lending, July 10, 2007, and such additional guidance applicable at the time of loan origination
- Substitution collateral may include cash and Treasury and agency securities as necessary to prudently manage the Cover Pool
- Mortgages must be current when they are added to the pool and any mortgages that become more than 60- days past due must be replaced
- Mortgages must be first lien only
- Mortgages must have a maximum loan-to-value ("LTV") of 80% at the time of inclusion in the Cover Pool
- A single Metro Statistical Area cannot make up more than 20% of the Cover Pool
- Negative amortization mortgages are not eligible for the Cover Pool
- Bondholders must have a perfected security interest in these mortgage loans.

Over- collateralization - Issuers must maintain an overcollateralization value at all times of at least 5% of the outstanding principal balance of the Covered Bonds (see "Asset Coverage Test").

For the purposes of calculating the minimum required overcollateralization in the Covered Bond, only the 80% portion of the updated LTV will be credited. If a mortgage in the Cover Pool has a LTV of 80% or less, the full outstanding principal value of the mortgage will be credited. If a mortgage has a LTV over 80%, only the 80% LTV portion of each loan will be credited (see Appendix A for examples).

Issuers must update the LTV of mortgages in the Cover Pool on a quarterly basis using a nationally-recognized, regional housing price index or other comparable measurement.

Currency - Covered Bonds may be issued in any currency.

Interest Type - Covered Bonds may either be fixed or floating instruments.

Interest Payment Swaps - Issuers may enter into one or more swap agreements or similar contractual arrangements at the time of issuance. The purpose of such agreements include:

- To provide scheduled interest payments on a temporary basis in the event the issuer becomes insolvent
- To mitigate any timing mismatch, to the extent applicable, between interest payments and interest income

These swap agreements must be with financially sound counterparties and the identity of the counterparties must be disclosed to investors.

Currency Swap - If a Covered Bond is issued in a different currency than the underlying Cover Pool (or Mortgage Bond, if applicable), the issuer shall employ a currency swap.

Specified Investment Contract - Issuers must enter into a deposit agreement, e.g., guaranteed investment contract, or other arrangement whereby the proceeds of Cover Pool assets are invested (any such arrangement, a "Specified Investment") at the time of issuance with or by one or more financially sound counterparties. Following a payment default by the issuer or repudiation by the FDIC as conservator or receiver, the Specified Investment should pay ongoing scheduled interest and principal payments so long as the Specified Investment provider receives proceeds of the Cover Pool assets at least equal to the par value of the Covered Bonds.

The purpose of the Specified Investment is to prevent an acceleration of the Covered Bond due to the insolvency of the issuer.

Cover Pool Disclosure - Issuers must make available descriptive information on the Cover Pool with investors at the time an investment decision is being made and on a monthly basis after issuance. The SEC's Regulation AB provides a helpful template for preparing pool level information, such as presenting summary information in tabular or graphical format and using appropriate groups or ranges.

Issuers must make this information available to investors no later than 30 days after the end of each month.

As the Covered Bond market develops, issuers should consider disclosing metrics on the Cover Pools from their prior Covered Bonds whenever a new issuance occurs.

Substitution - If more than 10% of the Cover Pool is substituted within any month or if 20% of the Cover Pool is substituted within any one quarter, the issuer must provide updated Cover Pool information to investors.

Issuer Disclosure - The depository institution and the SPV (if applicable) must disclose information regarding its financial profile and other relevant information that an investor would find material.

Asset Coverage Test - The issuer must perform an Asset Coverage Test on a monthly basis to ensure collateral quality and the proper level of overcollateralization and to make any substitutions that are necessary to meet the provisions of this template. The results of this Asset Coverage Test and the results of any reviews by the Asset Monitor must be made available to investors.

Asset Monitor - The issuer must designate an independent Asset Monitor to periodically determine compliance with the Asset Coverage Test of the issuer.

Trustee - The issuer must designate an independent Trustee for the Covered Bonds. Among other responsibilities, this Trustee must represent the interest of investors and must enforce the investors' rights in the collateral in the event of an issuer's insolvency.

Treatment of Covered Bond Proceeds - In the event of a default, any losses must be allocated pro rata across Covered Bond issuances that utilize a common Cover Pool, irrespective of the maturity of the individual issuances.

SEC Registration - Covered Bonds may be issued as registered securities or may be exempt from registration under securities laws. This template is not meant to address disclosure and other requirements for a security registered with the Securities and Exchange Commission.

Regulatory Authorization - *Issuers must receive consent to issue Covered Bonds from their primary federal regulator.* Upon an issuer's request, their primary federal regulator will make a determination based on that agencies policies and procedures whether to give consent to the issuer to establish a Covered Bond program. Only well-capitalized institutions should issue Covered Bonds.

As part of their ongoing supervisory efforts, primary federal regulators monitor an issuer's controls and risk management processes.

Issuance Limitations - Covered Bonds may account for no more than four percent of an issuers' liabilities after issuance.

Event of Breach of the Asset Coverage Test - If the Asset Coverage Test of the Covered Bond program is breached, the issuer has one month to correct such breach. If, after one month, the breach remains, the Trustee may terminate the Covered Bond program and principal and accrued interest will be returned to investors. While such a breach exists, the issuer may not issue any additional Covered Bonds.

Insolvency Procedures - As conservator or receiver for an insured depository institution (IDI), the FDIC has three options in responding to a properly structured Covered Bond transaction of the IDI:

1) continue to perform on the Covered Bond transaction under its terms;
2) pay-off the Covered Bonds in cash up to the value of the pledged collateral; or
3) allow liquidation of the pledged collateral to pay-off the Covered Bonds.

If the FDIC adopts the first option, it would continue to make the Covered Bond payments as scheduled. The second or third options would be triggered if the FDIC repudiated the transaction or if a monetary default occurred. In both cases, the par value of the Covered Bonds plus interest accrued to the date of the appointment of the FDIC as conservator or receiver would be paid in full up to the value of the collateral.

If the value of the pledged collateral exceeded the total amount of all valid claims held by the secured parties, this excess value or over collateralization would be returned to the FDIC, as conservator or receiver, for distribution as mandated by the Federal Deposit Insurance Act.

If there were insufficient collateral pledged to cover all valid claims by the secured parties, the amount of the claims in excess of the pledged collateral would be unsecured claims in the receivership.

VII. ILLUSTRATIVE DIRECT ISSUANCE

This diagram is meant to show what a potential structure could look like if the issuer of a Covered Bond were a depository institution. It is not intended to endorse a specific structure but rather serves an illustrative purpose. Issuers may develop other structures that are consistent with the template.

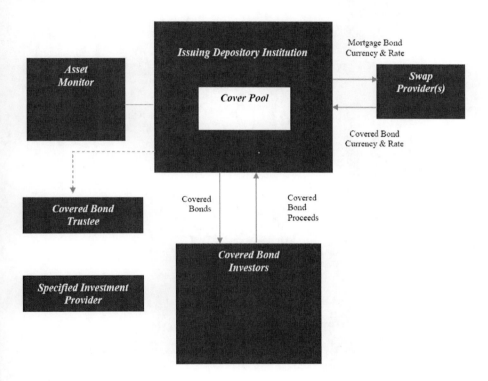

VIII. ILLUSTRATIVE SPV ISSUANCE

This diagram is meant to show what a potential structure could look like if the issuer of a Covered Bond were a SPV. It is not intended to endorse a specific structure but rather serves an illustrative purpose. Issuers may develop other structures that are consistent with the template.

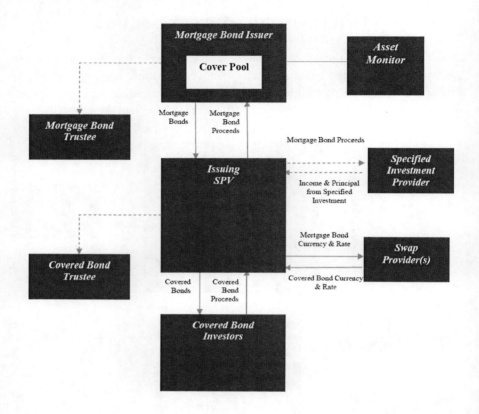

APPENDIX A: COVER POOL COLLATERALIZATION CALCULATION

As stated in Section VI., a minimum overcollateralization of 5% of the principal value of the Covered Bond must be maintained. Furthermore, mortgages must have a maximum LTV of 80% at the time of inclusion in the Cover Pool.

For the purposes of calculating the overcollateralization, 80% of the updated LTV will be credited towards the Cover Pool. For mortgages with an LTV of 80% or less, the full outstanding principal value will be credited. For mortgages with an LTV over 80%, only the 80% LTV portion of each loan will be credited.

This appendix provides examples of how loans may be credited against the required collateral of the Cover Pool.

ILLUSTRATIVE ASSUMPTIONS:

- $1,000 Covered Bond issuance
- Minimum overcollateralization of 5%
- Updated maximum LTV of 80% credited toward overcollateralization - $1,050 of required collateral ($1,000 x 1.05)

Scenario A:
- Pool of $80 loans on homes with an updated value of $100
- $1,050 / ($80 x 1.0) = 13.125 loans required in Cover Pool

Scenario B:
- Pool of $60 loans on homes with an updated value of $100
- $1,050 / ($60 x 1.0) = 17.500 loans required in Cover Pool

Scenario C:
- Pool of $80 loans on homes with an updated value of $80
- $1,050 / ($80 x 0.8) = 16.406 loans required in Cover Pool

APPENDIX B: FINAL FDIC COVERED BOND POLICY STATEMENT

FEDERAL DEPOSIT INSURANCE CORPORATION
Covered Bond Policy Statement
AGENCY: Federal Deposit Insurance Corporation (FDIC).
ACTION: Final Statement of Policy

SUMMARY: The Federal Deposit Insurance Corporation (the FDIC) is publishing a final policy statement on the treatment of covered bonds in a conservatorship or receivership. This policy statement provides guidance on the availability of expedited access to collateral pledged for certain covered bonds after the FDIC decides whether to terminate or continue the transaction. Specifically, the policy statement clarifies how the FDIC will apply the consent requirements of section 11(e)(13)(C) of the Federal Deposit Insurance Act (FDIA) to such covered bonds to facilitate the prudent development of the U.S. covered bond market consistent with the FDIC's responsibilities as conservator or receiver for insured depository institutions (IDI). As the U.S.

128   The Department of the Treasury

covered bond market develops, future modifications or amendments may be considered by the FDIC.

FOR FURTHER INFORMATION CONTACT: Richard T. Aboussie, Associate General Counsel, Legal Division (703) 562-2452; Michael H. Krimminger, Special Advisor for Policy (202) 898-8950.

SUPPLEMENTARY INFORMATION

I. Background

On April 23, 2008, the FDIC published the Interim Final Covered Bond Policy Statement for public comment. 73 FR 21949 (April 23, 2008). After carefully reviewing and considering all comments, the FDIC has adopted certain limited revisions and clarifications to the Interim Policy Statement (as discussed in Part II) in the Final Policy Statement.[6]

Currently, there are no statutory or regulatory prohibitions on the issuance of covered bonds by U.S. banks. Therefore, to reduce market uncertainty and clarify the application of the FDIC's statutory authorities for U.S. covered bond transactions, the FDIC issued an Interim Policy Statement to provide guidance on the availability of expedited access to collateral pledged for certain covered bonds by IDIs in a conservatorship or a receivership. As discussed below, under section 11(e)(13)(C) of the FDIA, any liquidation of collateral of an IDI placed into conservatorship or receivership requires the consent of the FDIC during the initial 45 days or 90 days after its appointment, respectively. Consequently, issuers of covered bonds have incurred additional costs from maintaining additional liquidity needed to insure continued payment on outstanding bonds if the FDIC as conservator or receiver fails to make payment or provide access to the pledged collateral during these periods after any decision by the FDIC to terminate the covered bond transaction. The Policy Statement does not impose any new obligations on the FDIC, as conservator or receiver, but does define the circumstances and the specific covered bond transactions for which the FDIC will grant consent to expedited access to pledged covered bond collateral.

Covered bonds are general, non-deposit obligation bonds of the issuing bank secured by a pledge of loans that remain on the bank's balance sheet. Covered bonds originated in Europe, where they are subject to extensive statutory and supervisory regulation designed to protect the interests of covered bond investors from the risks of insolvency of the issuing bank. By contrast, covered bonds are a relatively new innovation in the U.S. with only two issuers to date: Bank of America, N.A. and Washington Mutual. These initial U.S. covered bonds were issued in September 2006.

In the covered bond transactions initiated in the U.S. to date, an IDI sells mortgage bonds, secured by mortgages, to a trust or similar entity ("special purpose vehicle" or "SPV").[7] The pledged mortgages remain on the IDI's balance sheet, securing the IDI's obligation to make payments on the debt, and the SPV sells covered bonds, secured by the mortgage bonds, to investors. In the event of a default by the IDI, the mortgage bond trustee takes possession of the pledged mortgages and continues to make payments to the SPV to service the covered bonds. Proponents argue that covered bonds provide new and additional sources of liquidity and diversity to an institution's funding base.

The FDIC agrees that covered bonds may be a useful liquidity tool for IDIs as part of an overall prudent liquidity management framework and within the parameters set forth in the Policy Statement. While covered bonds, like other secured liabilities, could increase the costs to the deposit insurance fund in a receivership, these potential costs must be balanced with diversification of sources of liquidity and the benefits that accrue from additional on-balance sheet alternatives to securitization for financing mortgage lending. The Policy Statement seeks to balance these considerations by clarifying the conditions and circumstances under which the FDIC will grant automatic consent to access pledged covered bond collateral. The FDIC believes that the prudential limitations set forth in the Policy Statement permit the incremental development of the covered bond market, while allowing the FDIC, and other regulators, the opportunity to evaluate these transactions within the U.S. mortgage market. In fulfillment of its responsibilities as deposit insurer and receiver for failed IDIs, the FDIC will continue to review the development of the covered bond marketplace in the U.S. and abroad to gain further insight into the appropriate role of covered bonds in IDI funding and the U.S. mortgage market, and their potential consequences for the deposit insurance fund. (For ease of reference, throughout this discussion, when we refer to "covered bond obligation," we are referring to the part of the covered bond transaction comprising the IDI's debt obligation, whether to the SPV, mortgage bond trustee, or other parties; and "covered bond obligee" is the entity to which the IDI is indebted.)

Under the FDIA, when the FDIC is appointed conservator or receiver of an IDI, contracting parties cannot terminate agreements with the IDI because of the insolvency itself or the appointment of the conservator or receiver. In addition, contracting parties must obtain the FDIC's consent during the forty-five day period after appointment of FDIC as conservator, or during the ninety

130 The Department of the Treasury

day period after appointment of FDIC as receiver before, among other things, terminating any contract or liquidating any collateral pledged for a secured transaction.[8] During this period, the FDIC must still comply with otherwise enforceable provisions of the contract. The FDIC also may terminate or repudiate any contract of the IDI within a reasonable time after the FDIC's appointment as conservator or receiver if the conservator or receiver determines that the agreement is burdensome and that the repudiation will promote the orderly administration of the IDI's affairs.[9]

As conservator or receiver for an IDI, the FDIC has three options in responding to a properly structured covered bond transaction of the IDI: 1) continue to perform on the covered bond transaction under its terms; 2) pay-off the covered bonds in cash up to the value of the pledged collateral; or 3) allow liquidation of the pledged collateral to pay-off the covered bonds. If the FDIC adopts the first option, it would continue to make the covered bond payments as scheduled. The second or third options would be triggered if the FDIC repudiated the transaction or if a monetary default occurred. In both cases, the par value of the covered bonds plus interest accrued to the date of the appointment of the FDIC as conservator or receiver would be paid in full up to the value of the collateral. If the value of the pledged collateral exceeded the total amount of all valid claims held by the secured parties, this excess value or over collateralization would be returned to the FDIC, as conservator or receiver, for distribution as mandated by the FDIA. On the other hand, if there were insufficient collateral pledged to cover all valid claims by the secured parties, the amount of the claims in excess of the pledged collateral would be unsecured claims in the receivership.

While the FDIC can repudiate the underlying contract, and thereby terminate any continuing obligations under that contract, the FDIA prohibits the FDIC, as conservator or receiver from avoiding any legally enforceable or perfected security interest in the assets of the IDI unless the interest was taken in contemplation of the IDI's insolvency or with the intent to hinder, delay, or defraud the IDI or its creditors.[10] This statutory provision ensures protection for the valid claims of secured creditors up to the value of the pledged collateral. After a default or repudiation, the FDIC as conservator or receiver may either pay resulting damages in cash up to the value of the collateral or turn over the collateral to the secured party for liquidation. For example, if the conservator or receiver repudiated a covered bond transaction, as discussed in Part II below, it would pay damages limited to par value of the covered bonds and accrued interest up to the date of appointment of the conservator or receiver, if sufficient collateral was in the cover pool, or turn over the collateral for liquidation with the conservator or receiver recovering any proceeds in excess of those damages. In liquidating any collateral for a covered bond transaction, it would be essential that the secured party liquidate the collateral in a commercially reasonable and expeditious manner taking into account the then-existing market conditions.

As noted above, existing covered bond transactions by U.S. issuers have used SPVs. However, nothing in the Policy Statement requires the use of an SPV. Some questions have been posed about the treatment of a subsidiary or SPV after appointment of the FDIC as conservator or receiver. The FDIC applies well-defined standards to determine whether to treat such entities as "separate" from the IDI. If a subsidiary or SPV, in fact, has fulfilled all requirements for treatment as a "separate" entity under applicable law, the FDIC as conservator or receiver has not applied its statutory powers to the subsidiary's or SPV's contracts with third parties. While the determination of whether a subsidiary or SPV has been organized and maintained as a separate entity from the IDI must be determined based on the specific facts and circumstances, the standards for such decisions are set forth in generally applicable judicial decisions and in the FDIC's regulation governing subsidiaries of insured state banks, 12 C.F.R. § 362.4.

The requests to the FDIC for guidance have focused principally on the conditions under which the FDIC would grant consent to obtain collateral for a covered bond transaction before the expiration of the forty-five day period after appointment of a conservator or the ninety day period after appointment of a receiver. IDIs interested in issuing covered bonds have expressed concern that the requirement to seek the FDIC's consent before exercising on the collateral after a breach could interrupt payments to the covered bond obligee for as long as 90 days. IDIs can provide for additional liquidity or other hedges to accommodate this potential risk to the continuity of covered bond payments but at an additional cost to the transaction. Interested parties requested that the FDIC provide clarification about how FDIC would apply the consent requirement with respect to covered bonds. Accordingly, the FDIC has determined to issue this Final Covered Bond Policy Statement in order to provide covered bond issuers with final guidance on how the FDIC will treat covered bonds in a conservatorship or receivership.

II. Overview of the Comments

The FDIC received approximately 130 comment letters on the Interim Policy Statement; these included comments from national banks, Federal Home Loan Banks, industry groups and individuals.

Most commenters encouraged the FDIC to adopt the Policy Statement to clarify how the FDIC would treat covered bonds in the case of a conservatorship or receivership and, thereby, facilitate the development of the U.S. covered bond market. The more detailed comments focused on one or more of the following categories of issues: (1) the FDIC's discretion regarding covered bonds that do not comply with the Policy Statement; (2) application to covered bonds completed prior to the Policy Statement; (3) the limitation of the Policy Statement to covered bonds not exceeding 4 percent of liabilities; (4) the eligible collateral for the cover pools; (5) the measure of damages provided in the event of default or repudiation; (6) the covered bond term limit; and (7) federal home loan bank advances and assessments.

Certain banks and industry associations sought clarification about the treatment of covered bonds that do not comply with the Policy Statement by the FDIC as conservator or receiver. Specifically, commenters asked the FDIC to clarify that if a covered bond issuance is not in conformance with the Policy Statement, the FDIC retains discretion to grant consent prior to expiration of the 45 or 90 day period on a case-by-case basis. Under Section 11(e)(13)(C) of the FDIA, the exercise of any right or power to terminate, accelerate, declare a default, or otherwise affect any contract of the IDI, or to take possession of any property of the IDI, requires the consent of the conservator or receiver, as appropriate, during the 45-day period or 90-day period after the date of the appointment of the conservator or receiver, as applicable. By the statutory terms, the conservator or receiver retains the discretion to give consent on a case-by-case basis after evaluation by the FDIC upon the failure of the issuer.

Comments from banks who issued covered bonds prior to the Policy Statement requested either 'grandfathering' of preexisting covered bonds or an advance determination by the FDIC before any appointment of a conservator or receiver that specific preexisting covered bonds qualified under the Policy Statement. After carefully considering the comments, the FDIC has determined that to 'grandfather' or otherwise permit mortgages or other collateral that does not meet the specific requirements of the Policy Statement to support covered bonds would not promote stable and resilient covered bonds as encompassed within the Policy Statement. If preexisting covered bonds, and their collateral, otherwise qualify under the standards specified in the Policy Statement, those covered bonds would be eligible for the expedited access to collateral provided by the Policy Statement.

A number of commenters requested that the limitation of eligible covered bonds to no more than 4 percent of an IDI's total liabilities should be removed or increased. Commenters also noted that other countries applying a cap have based the limitation on assets, not liabilities. The Policy Statement applies to covered bond issuances that comprise no more than 4 percent of an institution's total liabilities since, in part, as the proportion of secured liabilities increases the unpledged assets available to satisfy the claims of the Deposit Insurance Fund, uninsured depositors and other creditors decreases. As a result, the FDIC must focus on the share of an IDI's liabilities that are secured by collateral and balance the additional potential losses in the failure of an IDI against the benefits of increased liquidity for open institutions. The 4 percent limitation under the Policy Statement is designed to permit the FDIC, and other regulators, an opportunity to evaluate the development of the covered bond market within the financial system of the United States, which differs in many respects from that in other countries deploying covered bonds. Consequently, while changes may be considered to this limitation as the covered bond market develops, the FDIC has decided not to make any change at this time.

A number of commenters sought expansion of the mortgages defined as "eligible mortgages" and the expansion of collateral for cover pools to include other assets, such as second-lien home equity loans and home equity lines of credit, credit card receivables, mortgages on commercial properties, public sector debt, and student loans. Other commenters requested that "eligible mortgages" should be defined solely by their loan-to-value (LTV) ratios. After considering these comments, the FDIC has determined that its interests in efficient resolution of IDIs, as well as in the initial development of a resilient covered bond market that can provide reliable liquidity for well-underwritten mortgages, support retention of the limitations on collateral for qualifying covered bonds in the Interim Policy Statement. Recent market experience demonstrates that many mortgages that would not qualify under the Policy Statement, such as low documentation mortgages, have declined sharply in value as credit conditions have deteriorated. Some of the other assets proposed are subject to substantial volatility as well, while others would not specifically support additional liquidity for well-underwritten residential mortgages. As noted above, certain provisions of the Policy Statement may be reviewed and reconsidered as the U.S. covered bond market develops.

With regard to the comments that LTV be used as a guide to determine an "eligible mortgage," the FDIC does not believe that LTV can substitute for strong underwriting criteria to ensure sustainable mortgages. In response to the comments, and the important role that LTV plays in mortgage analysis, the Policy Statement will urge issuers to disclose LTV for mortgages in the cover pool to enhance transparency for the covered bond market and promote stable cover pools. However, no specific LTV limitation will be imposed.

Two commenters suggested that the Policy Statement should be clarified to permit the substitution of cash as cover pool collateral. The Policy Statement has been modified to allow for the substitution of cash and Treasury and agency securities. The substitution of such collateral does not impair the strength of the cover pool and may be an important tool to limit short-term strains on issuing IDIs if eligible mortgages or AAA-rated mortgage securities must be withdrawn from the cover pool.

A number of commenters requested guidance on the calculation of damages the receiver will pay to holders of covered bonds in the case of repudiation or default. Under 12 USC § 1821(e)(3), the liability of the conservator or receiver for the disaffirmance or repudiation of any contract is limited to "actual direct compensatory damages" and determined as of the date of appointment of the conservator or receiver. In the repudiation of contracts, such damages generally are defined by the amount due under the contract repudiated, but excluding any amounts for lost profits or opportunities, other indirect or contingent claims, pain and suffering, and exemplary or punitive damages. Under the Policy Statement, the FDIC agrees that "actual direct compensatory damages" due to bondholders, or their representative(s), for repudiation of covered bonds will be limited to the par value of the bonds plus accrued interest as of the date of appointment of the FDIC as conservator or receiver. The FDIC anticipates that IDIs issuing covered bonds, like other obligations bearing interest rate or other risks, will undertake prudent hedging strategies for such risks as part of their risk management program.

Many commenters suggested that the 10-year term limit should be removed to permit longer-term covered bond maturities. After reviewing the comments, the FDIC agrees that longer-term covered bonds should not pose a significant, additional risk and may avoid short-term funding volatility. Therefore, the FDIC has revised the Interim Policy Statement by increasing the term limit for covered bonds from 10 years to 30 years.

A number of the Federal Home Loan Banks, and their member institutions, objected to the inclusion of FHLB advances in the definition of "secured liabilities," any imposed cap on such advances, and any change in

Best Practices for Residential Covered Bonds 135

assessment rates. Under 12 C.F.R. Part 360.2 (Federal Home Loan Banks as Secured Creditors), secured liabilities include loans from the Federal Reserve Bank discount window, Federal Home Loan Bank (FHLB) advances, repurchase agreements, and public deposits. However, the Policy Statement does not impose a cap on FHLB advances and has no effect on an IDI's ability to obtain FHLB advances or its deposit insurance assessments. The Policy Statement solely addresses covered bonds.

However, as noted above, where an IDI relies very heavily on secured liabilities to finance its lending and other business activities, it does pose a greater risk of loss to the Deposit Insurance Fund in any failure. Should the covered bond market develop as a significant source of funding for IDIs, and should that development create substantial increases in an IDI's reliance on secured funding, it would increase the FDIC's losses in a failure and perhaps outweigh the benefits of improved liquidity. As a result, it is appropriate for the FDIC to consider the risks of such increased losses. Consideration of these risks may occur in a possible future request for comments on secured liabilities, but they are not addressed in this Policy Statement.

III. Final Statement of Policy

For the purposes of this final Policy Statement, a "covered bond" is defined as a non-deposit, recourse debt obligation of an IDI with a term greater than one year and no more than thirty years, that is secured directly or indirectly by a pool of eligible mortgages or, not exceeding ten percent of the collateral, by AAA-rated mortgage bonds. The term "covered bond obligee" is the entity to which the IDI is indebted.

To provide guidance to potential covered bond issuers and investors, while allowing the FDIC to evaluate the potential benefits and risks that covered bond transactions may pose to the deposit insurance fund in the U.S. mortgage market, the application of the policy statement is limited to covered bonds that meet the following standards.

This Policy Statement only applies to covered bond issuances made with the consent of the IDI's primary federal regulator in which the IDI's total covered bond obligations at such issuance comprise no more than 4 percent of an IDI's total liabilities. The FDIC is concerned that unrestricted growth while the FDIC is evaluating the potential benefits and risks of covered bonds could excessively increase the proportion of secured liabilities to unsecured liabilities. The larger the balance of secured liabilities on the balance sheet, the smaller the value of assets that are available to satisfy depositors and general creditors, and consequently the greater the potential loss to the Deposit Insurance Fund. To address these concerns, the policy statement is limited to covered bonds that comprise no more than 4 percent of a financial institution's total liabilities after issuance.

In order to limit the risks to the deposit insurance fund, application of the Policy Statement is restricted to covered bond issuances secured by perfected security interests under applicable state and federal law on performing eligible mortgages on one-to-four family residential properties, underwritten at the fully indexed rate and relying on documented income, a limited volume of AAA-rated mortgage securities, and certain substitution collateral. The Policy Statement provides that the mortgages shall be underwritten at the fully indexed rate relying on documented income, and comply with existing supervisory guidance governing the underwriting of residential mortgages, including the Interagency Guidance on Non-Traditional Mortgage Products, October 5, 2006, and the Interagency.

Statement on Subprime Mortgage Lending, July 10, 2007, and such additional guidance applicable at the time of loan origination. In addition, the Policy Statement requires that the eligible mortgages and other collateral pledged for the covered bonds be held and owned by the IDI. This requirement is designed to protect the FDIC's interests in any over collateralization and avoid structures involving the transfer of the collateral to a subsidiary or SPV at initiation or prior to any IDI default under the covered bond transaction.

The FDIC recognizes that some covered bond programs include mortgage-backed securities in limited quantities. Staff believes that allowing some limited inclusion of AAA-rated mortgage-backed securities as collateral for covered bonds during this interim, evaluation period will support enhanced liquidity for mortgage finance without increasing the risks to the deposit insurance fund. Therefore, covered bonds that include up to 10 percent of their collateral in AAA-rated mortgage securities backed solely by mortgage loans that are made in compliance with guidance referenced above will meet the standards set forth in the Policy Statement. In addition, substitution collateral for the covered bonds may include cash and Treasury and agency securities as necessary to prudently manage the cover pool. Securities backed by tranches in other securities or assets (such as Collateralized Debt Obligations) are not considered to be acceptable collateral.

The Policy Statement provides that the consent of the FDIC, as conservator or receiver, is provided to covered bond obligees to exercise their contractual rights over collateral for covered bond transactions conforming to

Best Practices for Residential Covered Bonds

the Interim Policy Statement no sooner than ten (10) business days after a monetary default on an IDI's obligation to the covered bond obligee, as defined below, or ten (10) business days after the effective date of repudiation as provided in written notice by the conservator or receiver.

The FDIC anticipates that future developments in the marketplace may present interim final covered bond structures and structural elements that are not encompassed within this Policy Statement and therefore the FDIC may consider future amendment (with appropriate notice) of this Policy Statement as the U.S. covered bond market develops.

IV. Scope and Applicability

This Policy Statement applies to the FDIC in its capacity as conservator or receiver of an insured depository institution.

This Policy Statement only addresses the rights of the FDIC under 12 U.S.C. § 1821(e)(13)(C). A previous policy statement entitled "Statement of Policy on Foreclosure Consent and Redemption Rights," August 17, 1992, separately addresses consent under 12 U.S.C. § 1825(b), and should be separately consulted.

This Policy Statement does not authorize, and shall not be construed as authorizing, the waiver of the prohibitions in 12 U.S.C. § 1825(b)(2) against levy, attachment, garnishment, foreclosure or sale of property of the FDIC, nor does it authorize or shall it be construed as authorizing the attachment of any involuntary lien upon the property of the FDIC. The Policy Statement provides that it shall not be construed as waiving, limiting or otherwise affecting the rights or powers of the FDIC to take any action or to exercise any power not specifically mentioned, including but not limited to any rights, powers or remedies of the FDIC regarding transfers taken in contemplation of the institution's insolvency or with the intent to hinder, delay or defraud the institution or the creditors of such institution, or that is a fraudulent transfer under applicable law.

The Board of Directors of the FDIC has adopted a final Covered Bond Policy Statement. The text of the Covered Bond Policy Statement follows:

138   The Department of the Treasury

Covered Bond Policy Statement

Background

Insured depository institutions ("IDIs") are showing increasing interest in issuing covered bonds. Although covered bond structures vary, in all covered bonds the IDI issues a debt obligation secured by a pledge of assets, typically mortgages. The debt obligation is either a covered bond sold directly to investors, or mortgage bonds which are sold to a trust or similar entity ("special purpose vehicle" or "SPV") as collateral for the SPV to sell covered bonds to investors. In either case, the IDI's debt obligation is secured by a perfected first priority security interest in pledged mortgages, which remain on the IDI's balance sheet. Proponents argue that covered bonds provide new and additional sources of liquidity and diversity to an institution's funding base. Based upon the information available to date, the FDIC agrees that covered bonds may be a useful liquidity tool for IDIs as part of an overall prudent liquidity management framework and the parameters set forth in this policy statement. Because of the increasing interest IDIs have in issuing covered bonds, the FDIC has determined to issue this policy statement with respect to covered bonds.

(a) Definitions.

(1) For the purposes of this policy statement, a "covered bond" shall be defined as a non-deposit, recourse debt obligation of an IDI with a term greater than one year and no more than thirty years, that is secured directly or indirectly by perfected security interests under applicable state and federal law on assets held and owned by the IDI consisting of eligible mortgages, or AAA-rated mortgage-backed securities secured by eligible mortgages if for no more than ten percent of the collateral for any covered bond issuance or series. Such covered bonds may permit substitution of cash and United States Treasury and agency securities for the initial collateral as necessary to prudently manage the cover pool.

(2) The term "eligible mortgages" shall mean performing first-lien mortgages on one-to-four family residential properties, underwritten at the fully indexed rate[11] and relying on documented income, and complying with existing supervisory guidance governing the underwriting of residential mortgages, including the Interagency Guidance on Non-Traditional Mortgage Products, October 5, 2006, and the Interagency Statement on Subprime Mortgage Lending, July 10, 2007, and such additional guidance applicable at the time of loan origination. Due to the predictive quality of loan-to-value ratios in evaluating residential mortgages, issuers should disclose loan-to-

Best Practices for Residential Covered Bonds

value ratios for the cover pool to enhance transparency for the covered bond market.

(3) The term "covered bond obligation," shall be defined as the portion of the covered bond transaction that is the insured depository institution's debt obligation, whether to the SPV, mortgage bond trustee, or other parties.

(4) The term "covered bond obligee" is the entity to which the insured depository institution is indebted.

(5) The term "monetary default" shall mean the failure to pay when due (taking into account any period for cure of such failure or for forbearance provided under the instrument or in law) sums of money that are owed, without dispute, to the covered bond obligee under the terms of any bona fide instrument creating the obligation to pay.

(6) The term "total liabilities" shall mean, for banks that file quarterly Reports of Condition and Income (Call Reports), line 21 "Total liabilities" (Schedule RC); and for thrifts that file quarterly Thrift Financial Reports (TFRs), line SC70 "Total liabilities" (Schedule SC).

(b) Coverage. This policy statement only applies to covered bond issuances made with the consent of the IDI's primary federal regulator in which the IDI's total covered bond obligation as a result of such issuance comprises no more than 4 percent of an IDI's total liabilities, and only so long as the assets securing the covered bond obligation are eligible mortgages or AAA-rated mortgage securities on eligible mortgages, if not exceeding 10 percent of the collateral for any covered bond issuance, Substitution for the initial cover pool collateral may include cash and Treasury and agency securities as necessary to prudently manage the cover pool.

(c) Consent to certain actions. The FDIC as conservator or receiver consents to a covered bond obligee's exercise of the rights and powers listed in 12 U.S.C. § 1821(e)(13)(C), and will not assert any rights to which it may be entitled pursuant to 12 U.S.C. § 1821(e)(13)(C), after the expiration of the specified amount of time, and the occurrence of the following events:

(1) If at any time after appointment the conservator or receiver is in a monetary default to a covered bond obligee, as defined above, and remains in monetary default for ten (10) business days after actual delivery of a written request to the FDIC pursuant to paragraph (d) hereof to exercise contractual rights because of such monetary default, the FDIC hereby consents pursuant to 12 U.S.C. § 1821(e)(13)(C) to the covered bond obligee's exercise of any such contractual rights, including liquidation of properly pledged collateral by commercially reasonable and expeditious methods taking into account existing

market conditions, provided no involvement of the receiver or conservator is required.

(2) If the FDIC as conservator or receiver of an insured depository institution provides a written notice of repudiation of a contract to a covered bond obligee, and the FDIC does not pay the damages due pursuant to 12 U.S.C. § 1821(e) by reason of such repudiation within ten (10) business days after the effective date of the notice, the FDIC hereby consents pursuant to 12 U.S.C. § 1821(e)(13)(C) for the covered bond obligee's exercise of any of its contractual rights, including liquidation of properly pledged collateral by commercially reasonable and expeditious methods taking into account existing market conditions, provided no involvement of the receiver or conservator is required.

(3) The liability of a conservator or receiver for the disaffirmance or repudiation of any covered bond issuance obligation, or for any monetary default on, any covered bond issuance, shall be limited to the par value of the bonds issued, plus contract interest accrued thereon to the date of appointment of the conservator or receiver.

(d) Consent. Any party requesting the FDIC's consent as conservator or receiver pursuant to 12 U.S.C. § 1821(e)(13)(C) pursuant to this policy statement should provide to the Deputy Director, Division of Resolutions and Receiverships, Federal Deposit Insurance Corporation, 550 17th Street, NW, F-7076, Washington DC 20429-0002, a statement of the basis upon which such request is made, and copies of all documentation supporting such request, including without limitation a copy of the applicable contract and of any applicable notices under the contract.

(e) Limitations. The consents set forth in this policy statement do not act to waive or relinquish any rights granted to the FDIC in any capacity, pursuant to any other applicable law or any agreement or contract. Nothing contained in this policy alters the claims priority of collateralized obligations. Nothing contained in this policy statement shall be construed as permitting the avoidance of any legally enforceable or perfected security interest in any of the assets of an insured depository institution, provided such interest is not taken in contemplation of the institution's insolvency, or with the intent to hinder, delay or defraud the IDI or its creditors. Subject to the provisions of 12 U.S.C. § 1821(e)(13)(C), nothing contained in this policy statement shall be construed as permitting the conservator or receiver to fail to comply with otherwise enforceable provisions of a contract or preventing a covered bond obligee's exercise of any of its contractual rights, including liquidation of properly pledged collateral by commercially reasonable methods.

(f) No waiver. This policy statement does not authorize, and shall not be construed as authorizing the waiver of the prohibitions in 12 U.S.C. § 1825(b)(2) against levy, attachment, garnishment, foreclosure, or sale of property of the FDIC, nor does it authorize nor shall it be construed as authorizing the attachment of any involuntary lien upon the property of the FDIC. Nor shall this policy statement be construed as waiving, limiting or otherwise affecting the rights or powers of the FDIC to take any action or to exercise any power not specifically mentioned, including but not limited to any rights, powers or remedies of the FDIC regarding transfers taken in contemplation of the institution's insolvency or with the intent to hinder, delay or defraud the institution or the creditors of such institution, or that is a fraudulent transfer under applicable law.

(g) No assignment. The right to consent under 12 U.S.C. § 1821(e)(13)(C) may not be assigned or transferred to any purchaser of property from the FDIC, other than to a conservator or bridge bank.

(h) Repeal. This policy statement may be repealed by the FDIC upon 30 days notice provided in the Federal Register, but any repeal shall not apply to any covered bond issuance made in accordance with this policy statement before such repeal.

By order of the Board of Directors
Dated at Washington, DC this---------day of--------, 2008.
Federal Deposit Insurance Corporation

Robert E. Feldman
Executive Secretary

End Notes

[1] European Covered Bond Council, December 2007.

[2] Ibid

[3] The FDIC's Final Covered Bond Policy Statement dated July 15, 2008 outlines specific actions that the FDIC will take during an insolvency or receivership if certain conditions are met. Italicized terms indicate provisions that are part of both the FDIC's statement and this Best Practices Template. However, these italicized terms are not meant to cover all of the provisions of the FDIC statement. Market participants should independently review the FDIC's statement to ensure conformity with all provisions.

[4] In addition to SPV programs with a single issuer, multiple depository institutions could potentially utilize a joint SPV to pool assets. Each issuer would be responsible for meeting appropriate requirements and receiving consent from its primary federal regulator.

[5] The fully indexed rate equals the index rate prevailing at origination plus the margin to be added to it after the expiration of an introductory interest rate. For example, assume that a loan with an initial fixed rate of 7% will reset to the six-month London Interbank Offered Rate (LIBOR) plus a margin of 6%. If the six-month LIBOR rate equals 5.5%, lenders should qualify the borrower at 11.5% (5.5% + 6%), regardless of any interest rate caps that limit how quickly the fully indexed rate may be reached.

[6] For ease of reference, the Interim Final Covered Bond Policy Statement, published on April 23, 2008, will be referred to as the Interim Policy Statement. The Final Covered Bond Policy Statement will be referred to as the Policy Statement.

[7] The FDIC understands that certain potential issuers may propose a different structure that does not involve the use of an SPV. The FDIC expresses no opinion about the appropriateness of SPV or so-called "direct issuance" covered bond structures, although both may comply with this Statement of Policy.

[8] See 12 U.S.C. § 1821(e)(13)(C).

[9] See 12 U.S.C. §§ 1821(e)(3) and (13). These provisions do not apply in the manner stated to "qualified financial contracts" as defined in Section 11(e) of the FDI Act. See 12 U.S.C. § 1821(e)(8).

[10] See 12 U.S.C. §1821(e) (12).

[11] The fully indexed rate equals the index rate prevailing at origination plus the margin to be added to it after the expiration of an introductory interest rate. For example, assume that a loan with an initial fixed rate of 7% will reset to the six-month London Interbank Offered Rate (LIBOR) plus a margin of 6%. If the six-month LIBOR rate equals 5.5%, lenders should qualify the borrower at 11.5% (5.5% + 6%), regardless of any interest rate caps that limit how quickly the fully indexed rate may be reached.

CHAPTER SOURCES

Chapter 1 - This is an edited, reformatted and augmented version of a Congressional Research Service publication, R41322, dated March 4, 2011.

Chapter 2 - This is an edited, reformatted and augmented version of a testimony given by Scott A. Stengel, before the U.S. House Subcommittee on Capital Markets and Government Sponsored Enterprises, Hearing on "Legislative Proposals to Create a Covered Bond Market in the United States" on March 11, 2011.

Chapter 3 - This is an edited, reformatted and augmented version of a testimony given by Bert Ely, before the U.S. House Subcommittee on Capital Markets and Government Sponsored Enterprises, Hearing on "Legislative Proposals to Create a Covered Bond Market in the United States" on March 11, 2011.

Chapter 4 - This is an edited, reformatted and augmented version of a testimony given by Tim Skeet, Board Member of the International Capital Market Association, before the U.S. House Subcommittee on Capital Markets and Government Sponsored Enterprises, Hearing on "Legislative Proposals to Create a Covered Bond Market in the United States" on March 11, 2011.

Chapter 5 - This is an edited, reformatted and augmented version of a testimony given by Ralph Daloisio, Managing Director, Natixis, on behalf of the American Securitization Forum, ASF Covered Bonds Subforum, before the U.S. House Subcommittee on Capital Markets and Government Sponsored Enterprises, Hearing on "Legislative Proposals to Create a Covered Bond Market in the United States" on March 11, 2011.

144 Chapter Sources

Chapter 6 - This is an edited, reformatted and augmented version of a testimony given by Stephen G. Andrews, Bank of Alameda, before the U.S. House Subcommittee on Capital Markets and Government Sponsored Enterprises, Hearing on "Legislative Proposals to Create a Covered Bond Market in the United States" on March 11, 2001.

Chapter 7 - This is an edited, reformatted and augmented version of a testimony given by Federal Deposit Insurance Corporation, before the U.S. House Subcommittee on Capital Markets and Government Sponsored Enterprises, Hearing on "Legislative Proposals to Create a Covered Bond Market in the United States" on March 11, 2011.

Chapter 8 - This is an edited, reformatted and augmented version of a U.S. Department of the Treasury publication, dated July, 2008.

INDEX

A

access, 8, 13, 29, 31, 55, 67, 74, 102, 109, 127, 128, 129, 133
accessibility, 80
accounting, 5, 8, 23
accounting standards, 5
administrators, 54
advocacy, viii, 27, 80
age, 96
agencies, viii, 5, 8, 15, 18, 34, 62, 65, 80, 105, 123
agriculture, 119
alters, 140
amortization, 52, 121
annual rate, 22
appetite, 63, 67, 68, 72, 86
arbitrage, 54
Armenia, 25
assessment, 17, 58, 65, 109, 111, 135
atmosphere, 62
attachment, 137, 141
audit, 43, 90, 92
Austria, 25
authorities, 40, 43, 74, 75, 83, 84, 92, 107, 110, 128
authority, 15, 16, 18, 40, 45, 54, 56, 58, 81, 82, 83, 84, 85, 88, 92, 106, 107
automobiles, 43
avoidance, 31, 140

B

bail, 62
bank debt, 13
bank failure, 10
bank financing, 119
banking, 8, 9, 15, 18, 23, 24, 32, 49, 50, 52, 71, 80, 87, 92, 97, 105, 108, 109, 110, 111
banking industry, 110
banking sector, 71
bankruptcy, vii, viii, 1, 5, 12, 27, 36, 37, 39, 42, 56, 66, 75, 104, 120
base, 24, 59, 67, 70, 72, 75, 86, 93, 116, 129, 138
basis points, 14, 71, 86
beneficial effect, 67
beneficiaries, 56
benefits, 6, 41, 48, 86, 97, 102, 129, 133, 135
bondholders, 2, 3, 5, 25, 26, 29, 30, 33, 34, 35, 36, 74, 83, 84, 89, 92, 111, 134
borrowers, 46, 48, 49, 50, 51, 53, 99
budget deficit, 24
Bulgaria, 25
business strategy, 32
businesses, 44, 48, 80

C

candidates, 43
capital markets, viii, 14, 22, 24, 80, 88
cash, 5, 27, 34, 36, 51, 57, 63, 67, 76,
    97, 98, 99, 103, 106, 117, 118, 121,
    124, 130, 134, 136, 138, 139
cash flow, 5, 27, 51, 57, 97, 103, 106,
    117, 118
Census, 60
central bank, 57, 62, 70, 77
certificate, 110
challenges, 23, 71, 116
children, 99
clarity, 10, 12, 108, 116
classes, 8, 16, 32, 35, 43, 46, 49, 52, 68,
    70, 72, 104, 115, 116
collaboration, 94
collateralization, 75, 105, 109, 121, 124,
    130, 136
Collateralized Debt Obligations, 136
commercial, 16, 22, 23, 31, 35, 38, 39,
    43, 46, 55, 66, 67, 69, 80, 86, 88,
    102, 119, 133
common rule, 54
communities, 95
community, viii, 31, 33, 47, 54, 95, 96,
    97, 98
comparative analysis, 20
compensation, 41
competition, 12, 28
complement, 12, 23, 32, 116
complexity, 7
compliance, 33, 43, 55, 90, 92, 123, 136
composition, 43
conflict, 26, 33, 83
conflict of interest, 26, 33, 83
conformity, 141
consensus, viii, 70, 80
consent, 13, 27, 56, 106, 123, 127, 128,
    129, 131, 132, 135, 136, 137, 139,
    140, 141
constituents, 73
construction, 7, 43, 50
consulting, 54

consumers, 23, 27, 62, 80, 97, 100
conviction, 29
cooking, 50
cooperation, 108
coordination, 81, 86
cost, 6, 16, 17, 22, 23, 24, 27, 28, 31, 32,
    35, 43, 46, 62, 74, 86, 90, 93, 96,
    97, 98, 100, 106, 111, 131
cost effectiveness, 74
credit creation, 81
credit market, 96
credit rating, 42, 51, 57, 62, 89
creditors, 2, 3, 10, 11, 26, 27, 30, 36, 58,
    65, 66, 74, 83, 89, 92, 98, 102, 103,
    104, 105, 106, 107, 110, 117, 130,
    133, 136, 137, 140, 141
creditworthiness, 47, 62
crises, 52, 68
crisis management, 78
culture, 99
cure, 17, 90, 139
currency, 85, 91, 122
current balance, 7
customers, 49, 95, 96, 114
Czech Republic, 25

D

database, 74
deficiencies, 90
deficiency, 37, 84
delegates, 54
delinquency, 22
democratization, 80
Denmark, 25, 68, 85
depository institutions, ix, 12, 13, 34, 52,
    109, 110, 111, 113, 114, 116, 127,
    138, 141
deposits, 9, 13, 28, 59, 62, 84, 93, 107,
    114, 135
depth, 48
derivatives, 9, 52
directives, 10, 14, 75, 93
disclosure, 65, 68, 109, 120, 123
distortions, 105

Index

distress, 57, 58
distribution, 72, 124, 130
District of Columbia, 22
diversification, 24, 49, 129
diversity, 49, 97, 129, 138
draft, 57
dream, 99

E

economic growth, 22, 39
economic theory, 10
education, viii, 80
election, 36, 37
eligibility criteria, 64, 65, 76
emergency, 81
employment, 99
energy, ix, 96
engineering, 73
environment, 22, 25
equipment, 43
equity, 16, 18, 22, 27, 35, 38, 43, 44, 49,
    55, 59, 88, 133
Europe, vii, viii, ix, 1, 2, 12, 14, 25, 26,
    27, 31, 33, 38, 53, 61, 62, 65, 67,
    68, 70, 73, 89, 93, 96, 97, 108, 116,
    119, 128
European Central Bank, 3, 14, 18, 20,
    33, 64, 77, 78
European Commission, 78
European market, 66
European Union (EU), 4, 14, 18, 20, 33,
    40, 62, 75, 76, 77, 78
evidence, 78
evolution, viii, 61
execution, 62
exercise, 26, 30, 81, 88, 132, 136, 137,
    139, 140, 141
exposure, ix, 2, 6, 62, 86, 101, 102

F

faith, 87
families, 23, 28, 35, 48

FAS, 8, 19
FDI, 83, 104, 105, 107, 111, 142
fear, 28, 71, 83, 89
fears, 84
federal government, 24, 28, 44
Federal Government, 44
federal law, 4, 13, 136, 138
Federal Register, 19, 94, 141
fencing, 75
financial condition, 50
financial crisis, 22, 50, 57, 58, 63, 64,
    81, 96, 99, 102, 106
financial difficulty, 50
financial instability, 57
financial institutions, 2, 3, 9, 22, 23, 24,
    25, 31, 32, 33, 63, 64, 69, 70, 98,
    102, 105, 111
financial intermediaries, 22, 48
financial markets, 24, 32, 39, 57, 64, 73,
    85, 102
financial records, 43
financial regulation, 74
financial sector, 82
financial support, 80
financial system, 14, 21, 22, 23, 24, 52,
    53, 68, 80, 87, 90, 94, 102, 111,
    119, 133
Finland, 25, 69
fiscal deficit, 94
fixed rate, 142
flex, 22
flexibility, 72, 91, 107, 111
fluctuations, 9
force, 26, 49, 89
foreclosure, 6, 50, 51, 137, 141
foreign banks, 34
formation, 92
France, 25, 67, 80, 85, 87
franchise, 49
freedom, 99
funds, 2, 3, 4, 26, 28, 37, 51, 52, 57, 62,
    68, 75, 77, 96

148   Index

G

GDP, 94
geography, 85
Germany, 25, 68, 78, 85, 87, 97, 99
government funds, 18
government intervention, 24
grants, 45
Greece, 25
growth, vii, ix, 1, 2, 22, 25, 52, 63, 86, 94, 98, 113, 117, 135
growth rate, 22
guidance, 7, 8, 13, 16, 25, 76, 83, 108, 121, 127, 128, 131, 134, 135, 136, 138
guidelines, 86

H

health, 7, 71
hedging, 7, 45, 134
height, 63, 72, 96
history, 23, 26, 93, 110, 119
home ownership, 99
homeowners, ix, 113, 116
homes, 46, 55, 127
homework, 65
homogeneity, 88, 108, 116, 119
House, v, vi, 15, 17, 19, 21, 22, 39, 41, 61, 79, 95, 101
housing, ix, 41, 46, 50, 88, 96, 99, 116, 122
Hungary, 25
hybrid, 63

I

ideal, 29
identification, 90
identity, 122
imbalances, 62, 88
IMF, 18, 19
immunity, 31, 56

income, 24, 28, 45, 74, 97, 121, 122, 136, 138
income tax, 28
incompatibility, 27
independence, 109
individuals, 48, 132
industries, 30
industry, viii, ix, 17, 39, 74, 78, 80, 93, 96, 99, 101, 132
inflation, 22
initiation, 136
institutions, 4, 6, 7, 9, 10, 27, 28, 31, 32, 34, 53, 54, 62, 64, 76, 80, 93, 96, 97, 98, 102, 108, 111, 113, 114, 116, 119, 123, 133, 134
interest rates, 9, 23, 86
interference, 111
International Monetary Fund, 18
intervention, 6, 13, 24, 70, 88
investment, ix, 12, 16, 25, 28, 31, 47, 53, 63, 75, 76, 78, 80, 84, 86, 88, 89, 90, 91, 99, 101, 104, 106, 111, 118, 122
investment bank, 78, 80
investments, 24, 28, 80, 81, 87, 90, 93, 102, 103, 105, 120
Ireland, 25, 78
isolation, 5
issues, vii, viii, ix, 9, 42, 61, 64, 65, 67, 69, 72, 81, 86, 87, 101, 109, 132, 138
Italy, 25

J

Japan, 119
job creation, 39
jurisdiction, 66, 119

L

landscape, 61, 86
Latvia, 25

Index

149

laws, 14, 25, 27, 37, 66, 67, 68, 110, 120, 123
lead, 49, 52, 54, 69, 98, 104, 105, 106, 111
leadership, 38, 80
legal protection, 53, 68
legislative proposals, 3
lending, 2, 8, 9, 19, 23, 32, 38, 45, 48, 50, 58, 68, 73, 114, 129, 135
liquid assets, 76
liquidate, 30, 84, 131
liquidity ratio, 77
Lithuania, 25
local government, 24, 35, 60
longevity, 93
low risk, 87, 96

M

magnitude, 43
majority, 72, 97, 121
management, 32, 51, 66, 75, 84, 90, 93, 129, 138
market access, 33, 63, 69
market discipline, 102, 106, 111
market segment, 69
market share, 93
market structure, 80, 85, 97
marketplace, 48, 99, 108, 129, 137
matter, iv, 72
measurement, 78, 122
membership, 87
memory, 88
metropolitan areas, 46
microeconomic incentives, 32
mission, viii, 33, 39, 54, 80, 114
misunderstanding, 29
modifications, 24, 128
moral hazard, 48, 105
mortgage-backed securities, 4, 13, 16, 19, 22, 28, 39, 118, 136, 138
motivation, 89

N

national origin, 97
Netherlands, 25, 87
New Zealand, 85
Norway, 25, 69, 87

O

officials, 12
operations, 33, 64, 103, 106, 110
opportunities, 63, 134
organize, 80
overhead costs, 51
oversight, 104, 108
ownership, 50, 96, 99
ownership structure, 96

P

pain, 134
participants, viii, 12, 21, 22, 25, 26, 47, 62, 78, 80, 111, 116, 117, 120, 141
password, 55
permit, 49, 50, 52, 94, 96, 129, 132, 133, 134, 138
playing, 28, 114
Poland, 25
policy, 2, 4, 12, 13, 22, 28, 39, 77, 81, 83, 84, 87, 94, 104, 105, 106, 120, 127, 135, 136, 137, 138, 139, 140, 141
policy issues, 22
policymakers, vii, 1, 6, 10, 22, 32, 93
pools, 15, 17, 23, 25, 35, 65, 66, 67, 68, 71, 77, 86, 87, 97, 103, 104, 109, 132, 133, 134
portfolio, 9, 45, 114, 117
Portugal, 25
potential benefits, 135
precedent, 25, 31
preferential treatment, 33
preparation, iv, viii, 62
President, 19

150 Index

price index, 122
principles, 66, 83, 87, 88, 91, 103, 111
professionals, 93
profit, 58, 63
profitability, 50, 67
proposition, 29
protection, vii, 1, 33, 49, 51, 75, 88, 89, 106, 110, 111, 118, 130
prudential regulation, 75
public policy, 111, 114
public sector, 16, 22, 23, 27, 35, 67, 73, 88, 93, 104, 119, 133
publishing, 127

R

race, 46
rating agencies, 49, 65, 78, 117
real estate, 38, 85, 119
reasoning, 92
reception, 89
recession, 22, 99
recognition, 68
recommendations, iv, 53, 74
recovery, 10, 21, 22, 23, 51, 70, 73, 104, 110
reform, 22, 46, 76
Reform, 39, 46, 94, 106
reforms, 110
regulations, 8, 15, 29, 38, 40, 42, 43, 68, 76, 111
regulatory agencies, 7, 8, 103
regulatory framework, 14, 29, 82, 94, 108
regulatory requirements, 33
repo, 23, 70, 75
reputation, 95
requirements, 6, 8, 11, 14, 16, 17, 19, 23, 33, 35, 52, 54, 55, 75, 76, 88, 92, 104, 107, 117, 120, 121, 123, 127, 131, 132, 141
reserves, 63, 77
resilience, 24, 82
resolution, 35, 36, 37, 46, 82, 83, 105, 109, 110, 133

resources, ix, 8, 57, 92, 96
response, 11, 87, 114, 134
restitution, 30
restoration, 63
restrictions, 110
retail, 80
retail deposit, 80
risk factors, 120
risk management, 32, 124, 134
risk profile, 75
risks, 4, 7, 9, 19, 23, 26, 27, 35, 65, 67, 83, 103, 104, 105, 109, 128, 134, 135, 136
Romania, 25
rules, 8, 13, 18, 36, 54, 74, 75, 76, 88, 99, 104
Russia, 25

S

safety, 48, 49, 50, 53, 54, 63, 103, 108, 109, 111
savings, 18, 28, 34, 86
scope, 13
Secretary of the Treasury, 15, 29, 33, 38, 40, 54, 55, 104, 113
securities, viii, 4, 5, 6, 7, 8, 16, 17, 24, 28, 29, 37, 39, 42, 44, 47, 75, 87, 88, 96, 120, 121, 123, 134, 136, 138, 139
securities firms, 39
security, viii, 4, 10, 13, 16, 17, 24, 34, 36, 38, 40, 42, 62, 66, 80, 88, 102, 117, 120, 121, 123, 130, 136, 138, 140
segregation, 66, 90
sellers, 8
Senate, 18, 39, 84, 94
service provider, 76, 117
shortage, 24
short-term liabilities, 9
showing, 69, 138
signals, 84
silver, 24
skin, 2, 6, 7, 24, 89

Index

small businesses, 22, 23, 24, 27, 28, 35
society, 86
solution, 62, 73, 76, 97
Spain, 25, 85
spending, 94
stability, 14, 53, 64, 82, 111
stakeholders, viii, 61, 78
standardization, 89
state, 4, 13, 16, 60, 62, 68, 131, 136, 138
states, 84
statistics, 19, 69, 72
statutes, 75
stress, 57, 58, 76, 82, 86, 90, 105
structure, 7, 9, 47, 62, 66, 80, 102, 116, 117, 119, 125, 142
style, 67
subsidy, 22, 102, 105
substitution, 134, 136, 138
substitutions, 123
supervision, 2, 3, 25, 29, 33, 35, 37, 40, 68, 74, 92
supervisor, 3
supervisors, 103
surplus, 36, 37
Sweden, 25, 87
Switzerland, 25
systemic risk, 22, 24, 32, 65

T

tax collection, 22
taxpayers, 10, 24, 36, 45, 57, 58, 64, 68, 73, 106
technology, viii, 43, 80, 93
thrifts, 139
trade, 53, 73, 102, 117
trade deficit, 53
tranches, viii, 42, 50, 136
transactions, 25, 72, 78, 103, 106, 109, 128, 129, 131, 135, 136
transparency, 7, 8, 9, 11, 24, 35, 65, 74, 89, 105, 134, 139
Treasury Secretary, ix, 54, 90, 96

treatment, ix, 2, 5, 8, 13, 30, 38, 39, 66, 73, 75, 76, 77, 82, 90, 93, 101, 105, 109, 127, 131, 132
triggers, 76, 106
turbulence, 14, 63
Turkey, 25

U

U.S. economy, 48, 53
U.S. Treasury, 28
Ukraine, 25
underwriting, 2, 6, 7, 24, 99, 109, 117, 121, 134, 136, 138
uniform, 29
uninsured, 107, 133
unions, 28
United Kingdom (UK), 25, 66, 76, 85, 87

V

vacuum, 27
variations, 2, 3
vehicles, 12
volatility, 27, 91, 133, 134

W

waiver, 137, 141
Washington, viii, 21, 36, 39, 81, 94, 108, 129, 140, 141
waste, 35
weakness, 82
Western Europe, 64
wholesale, 62
withdrawal, 9
worldwide, 74, 86

Y

yield, 14, 47, 91